*If Not Me,
Who?*

If Not Me, Who?

What One Man Accomplished In His Battle For Equality

WENDELL H. BAKER, SR.

■■■

EDITED BY

BRUCE A. GLASRUD & MILTON S. JORDAN

STEPHEN F. AUSTIN STATE UNIVERSITY PRESS
NACOGDOCHES, TEXAS

Copyright © 2014 by Bruce A. Glasrud and Milton S. Jordan

All rights reserved. Printed in the United States of America. No part of this book may be used or reproduced in any manner whatsover without writer permission except in the case of brief quotations embodied in critical articles or reviews.

For more information:
Stephen F. Austin State University Press
P.O. Box 13007 SFA Station
Nacogdoches, Texas 75962
sfapress@sfasu.edu
www.sfasu.edu/sfapress

Edited by Bruce A. Glasrud and Milton S. Jordan
Book design by Kirstie Linstrom

Distributed by Texas A&M Consortium
www.tamupress.com

LIBRARY OF CONGRESS CATALOGING-IN-PUBLICATION DATA

Glasrud, Bruce A. and Milton S. Jordan
If Not Me, Who? / Bruce A. Glasrud and Milton S. Jordan

p.cm.

ISBN: 978-1-62288-072-0

TABLE OF CONTENTS

Foreword by Bernadette Pruitt	7
Acknowledgements	11
Introduction: If Not Wendell H. Baker, Who? by Bruce A. Glasrud and Milton S. Jordan	13
Preface	23
Chapter 1: Family Background	24
Chapter 2: Family Expansion and Community Relationships	25
Chapter 3: Early School Experiences and Limitations, College Experiences	28
Chapter 4: College, Farm Deferment, Marriage and Army	32
Chapter 5: Return from Service in Japan, Completion of College, and First Job: Teaching High School	34
Chapter 6: School Desegregation and Applicable Attitudes	45
Chapter 7: Civil Rights Activities Begin: Job and Educational Progress	47
Chapter 8: Making a Difference by Political Involvement (Hospital Election, Election Official, Housing Project)	50
Chapter 9: Paving Streets, Voting the City "Wet"	54
Chapter 10: Changing Avenue F to Martin Luther King Avenue	56
Chapter 11: Electing County Commissioner	58
Chapter 12: County Agent Promotion	60
Chapter 13: Principal's Promotion	61
Chapter 14: Certifying Our Policemen and No More Dime-Store Books	62
Chapter 15: Huntsville Independent Schools: 4A or 5A?	63
Chapter 16: My One Conviction	65
Chapter 17: Firing Policewoman, Deneen Ford--For What?	67
Chapter 18: Integrating the Huntsville Memorial Hospital: Just Well Planned, That's All	68
Chapter 19: First Black City Council Person	70
Chapter 20: Constable Elected	71
Chapter 21: Elected Local Doctor to City Council	72
Chapter 22: Blacks on County Democratic Committee	73

Chapter 23: Opening a Prenatal Clinic	74
Chapter 24: The Swimming Pool Event	75
Chapter 25: "Juneteenth" as a Holiday	76
Chapter 26: Organization of Voter Groups	77
Chapter 27: The Million Man March	79
Civil Rights Activist: Wendell H. Baker, Sr.	
by Naomi W. Lede	83
Discovering an Extended Family	
by James A. Baker, III, with Steve Fiffer	110
Appendix 1: Points That Affect Me--My Goals and Resolutions	115
Appendix 2: Important Accomplishments	115
Appendix 3: Certificate of Appreciation	117
Appendix 4: State of Texas Certificates	117
Appendix 5: Texas National Resource Conservation	117
Commission (TNRCC)	117
Appendix 6: Certificates of Training	117
Appendix 7: Certificates of Recognition	118
Selected Bibliography	119
Index	122

FOREWORD

I first met Mr. Wendell Harold Baker in 1997 or 1998, when my fellow Greater Zion Missionary Baptist Church congregant, music teacher and gospel singer Diane Patrick, invited me to speak to her elementary-school students for a Black History Month program in New Waverly, Texas. At the program, Mr. Baker, then in his mid to late seventies, talked about his experiences as a civic leader and retired scientist. Baker's charisma and charm won over the hearts of the group of Black, Hispanic, and White primary children from the rural town just north of Huntsville. I quickly realized I was in the presence of someone very special. It also occurred to me that Baker was immensely proud of his important place in history as a World War II veteran, an educator, singer, scientist, and community activist. His name always came up in conversations about local Black history and civil rights. Longtime residents lauded his efforts to desegregate the city of Huntsville in the 1960s. All this enthralled me as a future research project but, regrettably, I had a dissertation to complete.

Several years later retired Texas Southern University provost and emerita director and distinguished professor of Transportation Studies Naomi Ledé, affectionately known to members of my sorority, Sigma Gamma Rho, Inc., as "Soror Ledé," invited me to serve on a Black history steering committee that sought to commemorate prominent African Americans in Huntsville and Walker County, beginning in February 2002. This inspired me to begin an ongoing research project on African American life and culture in my adopted city, with a concentration on the Baker and Williams families (the latter being the great-grandparents of Naomi Ledé). I worked with a number of influential Huntsville and Walker County residents, including Mr. Baker. For two years, Baker and I teamed up with Ledé and other phenomenal Huntsville civic leaders to conduct oral interviews, search garages and closets for old photographs, pull out obituaries, trigger the memories of seniors, and speak to groups around town, usually to request organizational papers and histories, for our project. A perfectionist, Soror Ledé assembled an impressive group of mostly retired schoolteachers that met every other Tuesday at city hall, chamber of commerce, or the Samuel Walker Houston Cultural Center—the former African American High School, and named for the educator, civic leader, and son of the former slave of legendary Sam Houston, and Reconstruction politician Joshua Houston—to discuss our plans and progress on completing the book. With the help of retired biology teacher Hattye Palmer Owens; the late Herma Owens Johnson, at the time, a retired librarian; the late Linda Peas, a former city clerk; retired County

Clerk James Patton; librarian Cheryl Spencer; retired educator Lucy Mae Willis; myself; Baker; and several others, the ad hoc committee persevered. Dr. Ledé published *Pathfinders: A History of the Pioneering Efforts of African Americans, Huntsville, and Walker County, Texas* in 2004.

From this treasured experience, I got to know quite well and grew to love the Baker family. For a decade, Mr. Wendell and Mrs. Augusta Baker opened their lovely home to me and my students, and allowed numerous Sam Houston State University student groups to conduct interviews, from classes and fraternities to journalists and political groups. I conducted my first interviews with Mr. Baker in 2003. From these first interviews, I began reconstructing a fascinating family history that stretched back to antebellum slavery. I also interviewed Mr. Baker's last surviving siblings, the late James "Pap" Baker of Los Angeles, a retired civil servant and World War II veteran, and retired beautician Leola Adams. I grew to know personally some members of the extended family, including in-law and United Methodist Church minister, Rev. Dr. James Lawson, the organizer of the Nashville Student Movement (NSM) of the 1960s Modern Civil Rights Movement. Rev. Lawson, whose son, an attorney and city judge, is married to Wendell and Augusta Baker's youngest daughter, television executive Cima Baker Lawson, spoke to several hundred people a decade ago on the campus of SHSU, thanks to Wendell H. Baker. Yes, I saw Mr. Baker and his family giants. Yes, I imaged the Baker family and Wendell Baker as fascinating research and book projects.

Actually, Wendell Baker became much more to me. A dear friend, mentor, and father figure, Wendell Baker seemed larger than life. Our conversations generally included his reflections on his life as well as his love for his wife and children. He loved his family, especially his children, grandchildren, and extended family. He loved what his parents and he and his wife had accomplished, especially with respect to the Baker offspring. The extended Baker family includes physicians, attorneys, computer scientists, scientists, educators, college professors, business owners, ranchers, college students, civil servants, nurses, businesspersons in corporate America, and innovative preteens. Most importantly, the Baker family values the rich history of their ancestors, including husband, father, and farmer Jesse Baker, Wendell Baker's biracial father who stood as a bridge between the races in early twentieth-century Huntsville as well as the link between two prominent families, one Black and one White. Mr. Wendell Baker proudly shared this knowledge with me as well. I could foresee a second book project and once again grew enchanted with this potential project. However, I had to finish my first book project based on my dissertation study of the Great Migration to Houston.

Mr. Baker talked about more than himself and his family. Another topic dear to his heart was his home, Huntsville, Walker County, Texas. Mr. Baker loved his community. Even while exhausted from prostate cancer treatments and immobile the last few years of his life, Baker talked mostly about the challenges his beloved birthplace still faced. The rising dropout rate among African American youths, particularly young men, along with the disproportionately miniscule number of technical, professional positions in the hands of African Americans in Walker County and Huntsville continued to trouble him. He also expressed frustration about the apathy among African American youths in the twenty-first century. Worried less about his own lasting legacy and more about the ways African American professionals could reach out to the poor, he never stopped fighting. He talked to schoolchildren and college students. He spoke to church groups. He pleaded with local politicians and civic leaders. He talked to anyone who would listen to his thoughts on Black Huntsville, the poor, the disabled, and the future. During President Obama's first election bid for president in 2008 and his 2012 reelection campaign, Baker pleaded with African Americans, from fraternity brothers and members of the NAACP, to church groups and people in the community, demanding that African Americans register people to vote, create car pools on election day, and teach young people the importance of political mobilization. He loved people, even when people, frustrated by his rhetoric and perceived arrogance, did not always love him.

I loved Mr. Baker. His love for family and community has inspired me for a decade. I especially treasured his confidence. Wendell Harold Baker believed African Americans could achieve anything and everything. Racism never scared Baker; racists never made him flinch. Influenced greatly by his father Jesse Baker, Baker understood that people had to love themselves first. He believed that God demanded this of us all. Mr. Baker felt compelled to do his part to convince people of this fact.

He did not just love Blacks. A Dr. W. E. B. Du Bois, Rev. James Lawson and Rev. Dr. Martin Luther King integrationist, he treasured his friends of other racial and ethnic groups and valued their help when it came. He believed that God created all men and women equally. Even if humanity did not always accept this as truth, Wendell Harold Baker knew this to be fact. This fact and faith guided him for nearly a century. It kept his marriage intact for nearly seventy years. It influenced his children's amazing life choices. It pushed many members of the Baker extended family to soar. Mostly, it pushed Wendell Baker to continuously press forward and hope for a better tomorrow for humanity, especially the working peoples and marginalized of Huntsville and Walker County.

Texas historian Bruce A. Glasrud and Rev. Milton S. Jordan's book therefore stands as a special tribute to the late great Wendell Harold Baker.

It sets out to teach new generations of young people that their civil liberties often came at great sacrifice. This volume also reminds us of the need to continue Mr. Baker's legacy and mission of civic activism. In addition, it attempts to teach a community and state that ordinary, extraordinary African Americans from Texas contributed greatly to the Long Civil Rights Movement. This volume reminds readers that sacrifices lead to resurrected renaissances. Mostly, this incredible study pays homage to a great man, one of the greatest men I have ever had the pleasure of knowing. It is my hope that this work sparks new scholarship on other Texans like Baker, incredible men and women who risked much for their offspring and offspring's offspring, as well as their beloved local communities. With the Baker family's permission, I hope to continue my work on Wendell Baker and the Baker family. Thank you Mr. Wendell H. Baker (and Mrs. Augusta Baker) for opening your hearts, souls, and bank account to your community. Thank you for caring and thank you for loving. We will always love you!

Bernadette Pruitt
Sam Houston State University
Huntsville, Texas

ACKNOWLEDGMENTS

This book grew from a series of discussions between the two co-editors, Bruce A. Glasrud and Milton S. Jordan, that began at a meeting of the West Texas Historical Association at Sul Ross State University in Alpine, Texas. Glasrud chanced to ask Jordan whether a copy of Huntsville, Texas African American leader Wendell Baker's self-published book, *If Not Me, Who*, could be located by Jordan, who together with his wife Anne, operated a book-selling business. Jordan noted that a copy was impossible to find which led Glasrud to say that we should republish it. The reasons were two-fold: first, Wendell Baker was a prominent civil rights activist in East Texas, and secondly, his written story should be further distributed. Jordan concurred, and we embarked on our mission.

Baker's autobiography covers his life from birth to eighty plus years of age. Both his life and his book were singularly critical achievements. Reprinting it would acknowledge that status. For help in putting the book together, we are indebted to many people, not the least of whom was Wendell Baker, who enthusiastically supported our effort. He even loaned us his only copy of the book. His wife, Augusta Baker, and other family members have provided much support. Daughter, Pamela Baker, son, Wendell Jr. and his wife Jerrine Baker, have been particularly helpful providing information and locating photos for this book. Sam Houston State University historian Bernadette Pruitt, who has been helpful in numerous ways, kindly agreed to write a Foreword for the book. Her colleague, Jeff Littlejohn, provided encouragement and support. Invaluable help in getting started came from Cheryl Spencer in Special Collections at the Newton Gresham Library at Sam Houston State and from University Archivist, Barbara Kievit Mason. Additional assistance came from colleagues associated with the East Texas Historical Association, including good friends O. L. Davis and Dan K. Utley as well as ETHA friend and director, M. Scott Sosebee.

This book includes materials from two other authors, and we thank them for permission to use those segments—retired Texas Southern University scholar Naomi W. Lede, whose work originally was also published in Baker's book, and political leader and consultant James A. Baker, who learned from Wendell Baker and his brother that they were distant cousins. We are also grateful to the editor/director at Stephen F. Austin State University Press, Kim Verhines. She listened, facilitated, and encouraged our efforts. We cannot overlook the help that we received from our respective wives, Anne Jordan and Pearlene Glasrud. They provided essential support typing, proof reading, giving computer advice and guidance, and showing remarkable patience. For any errors or omissions, of course, we remain responsible.

Bruce A. Glasrud, San Antonio, Texas
Milton S. Jordan, Georgetown, Texas

Mr. and Mrs. Scott Plummer, Wendell Baker's neighbors who gave him a computer and encouraged Baker to write his autobiography. Photo courtesy of the Baker family

IF NOT WENDELL BAKER, WHO?

Bruce A. Glasrud and Milton S. Jordan

In the spring of 1961, thirty-eight year old Wendell H. Baker, Sr., a black Huntsville, Texas high school science teacher, a respected and popular instructor, was called into the office of the Huntsville superintendent of schools and asked if he would sell his newly built home that was located near a proposed affluent white subdivision. Baker responded, "It is not for sale. I built it myself for my family."[1] Upon refusing this peremptory, race-based demand, he was informed that he would receive no contract to teach for the ensuing year. This demeaning treatment occurred after twelve years of diligent, responsible teaching for the Huntsville African American high school. Baker's refusal also cost him his second job as a weekend radio announcer where for a short time he worked alongside Dan Rather, then a student at Sam Houston State College. A little less than a year after the episode with the superintendent, Baker accepted a job with the Goodyear Tire and Rubber Company in Beaumont; he became the "Jackie Robinson" of the Gulf Coast oil and rubber industry (the first African American hired in the oil, gas, and chemical industry to a responsible, technical position). But the effects of the earlier racist demand did not leave him, and Baker went on to become an ardent civil rights leader and activist in Huntsville, Texas.

Wendell Baker's inspirational and courageous life spanned nearly eighty years of the twentieth and the first thirteen years of the twenty-first century; he died in the fall of 2013, one day short of his ninety-first birthday. A teacher, chemist, chemical engineer, civil rights activist, and charismatic leader, Baker led an exemplary life and pursued a successful career.

Born in 1922 in Cotton Creek in Walker County, near Huntsville, Wendell Baker's early life was spent on a small, 100 acre family-owned farm. Two years later the family moved to Pine Hill, a little closer to Huntsville. In order to pursue a decent education (not always available to blacks in rural Texas), Baker's parents sent him to live for two years in Galveston before returning to Huntsville. Upon returning to Huntsville, Baker completed elementary school and then enrolled in Samuel Walker Houston High School, an all-black school in segregated Huntsville from which, at the age of sixteen, he graduated with the second highest honors. Not allowed to attend Huntsville's Sam Houston State College, Baker worked for a time (ironically at that very college's cafeteria) prior to enrolling in 1940 at Samuel Huston College (now Huston-Tillotson University), an all-black four-year college in Austin, Texas. Thanks to his vocal and musical talent, he traveled with a sextet earning money for the college, and receiving tuition and expenses for himself.

Baker left Samuel Huston soon after Japan's Pearl Harbor attack on the United States in December, 1941. As he later phrased it, "my college days came to a screeching halt when the war broke out."[2] He was drafted by the U. S. Army but received a two-year work deferment to help with the family farm, by then a 300 acre operation, since two brothers already served in the armed forces. Following his two year deferment he joined the army in 1944, serving in the Army Medical Corps. Although not a pacifist, he did not believe he should be fighting with weapons for democracy when blacks were denied democratic (read just and equitable) treatment. He chose not to carry a weapon. His skills were useful in other ways to the army, yet he, and numerous other blacks in key positions, received no promotions. Baker started as a private and after service in several medical roles, he finished as a private.

Discharged from the military in 1946, Baker continued his education. Rather than re-enter Samuel Huston College, he enrolled in 1947 at the newly established Texas State University for Negroes in nearby Houston, Texas. With a dream of later attending Meharry Medical College, he majored in chemistry and earned his bachelor's degree in chemistry from TSUN (now Texas Southern University) in 1949. Baker, as so many other World War II veterans, benefitted from the recently enacted G.I. Bill. Upon graduation, Baker decided to seek a teaching job prior to going to Meharry because of his family responsibilities. However, as time went on the increased needs of his wife and children and his commitment to teaching kept him in Huntsville. Teaching science at all-black Samuel Walker Houston High School was a distinct challenge. When he started, almost no equipment for science existed at the school, and the facilities were noticeably inadequate. With the assistance of white science teachers at the white high school Baker acquired some of the necessary equipment and he became chair of the science department. In addition to teaching biology, chemistry, physics, and general science he also sponsored the glee club as well as other musical groups. In this regard he served as choir and band director and often drove the bus for field trips and interscholastic contests. Then, in the spring of 1961, after twelve years as an exemplary teacher and leader in the Huntsville Independent School District, he was denied a contract renewal. In essence, he was fired.

In the long run, for Baker and for the growth of racial justice in Huntsville, and particularly for the black community of Huntsville, perhaps his firing was a propitious moment. Baker ended up with a job which offered more for his career and a better salary than teaching. As Bernadette Pruitt put it, "his transformation from fired schoolteacher to chemical engineer not only tripled his salary, but also prompted his catapult into local activism."[3] In the spring of 1962 Wendell Baker was offered and accepted a position with the Goodyear Tire and Rubber Company of Beaumont, Texas. At

Goodyear he started his career as a quality control specialist and eventually became a chemical engineer. He enjoyed his work, and was very good at it. He paved the way for the hiring of other African Americans in responsible positions in the oil, gas, and chemical enterprises in the "Golden Triangle" of Southeast Texas. Baker decided to retire from Goodyear Tire and Rubber in 1984, when he was sixty-two years of age. He had accomplished much by that time, not the least of which was the accomplishment of his civic activism.

Soon after Wendell Baker began his employment at Goodyear he suffered ill-health, spent time in a hospital for surgery, and four months later resumed work. With time on his hands for contemplation, he determined that the second-rate status of blacks in Huntsville needed a champion—he became a black rights activist. In particular he emerged as a civil and political rights crusader on behalf of black and white Huntsville.

Baker's first major foray into activism was in the political realm. In Huntsville, as in the rest of Texas, few blacks voted. For years they had almost no effect on general elections since the all-white primary kept them from having a voice in the key election, the Democratic Party primary. But the 1944 U.S. Supreme Court decision, *Smith vs. Allwright*, declared the Texas white primary unconstitutional. Blacks still had difficulty voting due to the poll tax since many could not afford the money to pay the tax. Baker solicited community help to pay the taxes for indigent potential voters, but with little success. He and his wife started paying the poll taxes for black voters, and blacks in Huntsville and Walker County gradually began voting—their first objective was to defeat the racist county sheriff and they were successful. Baker also was influential in organizing the Walker County Voter's League in December, 1962, a group that engaged the black community in voting and other efforts at reform. These political efforts were further encouraged in 1965, during the Democratic presidency of Texan Lyndon B. Johnson, with enactment of the 1965 Voting Rights Act.

The lack of a political voice was not the only challenge facing the black Huntsville community; school desegregation became a vital objective. The 1954 U.S. Supreme Court decision, *Brown vs. Board of Education of Topeka*, determined that "separate but equal" schools were inherently unequal and unconstitutional. Of course, in Texas, the black schools were certainly not equal as Wendell Baker discovered as a student and as a teacher. With the support of the Walker County Voter's League, Baker worked to get the schools of Huntsville integrated. He started with the local college, Sam Houston State College, that would not admit him earlier in his life. He and members of the League located possible students who fit all other qualifications and urged them to apply. Finally in the fall of 1964, ten years after the *Brown* decision, a young black man, John Arthur Patrick was admitted to Sam Houston State College. It took longer to gain integration at the local public schools; the school board began with a gradual plan of integration in 1965. Finally complete integration was accomplished in Huntsville in1968, fourteen years after the *Brown* decision declared segregated schools unconstitutional. Baker's daughter was in the first group of black students admitted to the previously all white high school, and was the first African American to graduate from that school.

Black residents in Huntsville faced one other critical challenge, the white refusal to provide equitable service in the public accommodations of the city and county. To confront and overcome that situation Baker and other blacks received support from the local NAACP. But some ministers and a few other conservative black residents counseled against confrontation. They had many objections, some reasonable—such as fear of violent white retaliation and loss of jobs. Baker, though, had his supporters, especially among younger citizens who organized themselves as the Huntsville Action for Youth in 1965, shortened to HA-You. With many public school students, HA-You challenged segregation in Huntsville schools and businesses by boycotts, by protest marches, and by sit-ins. White and black students from colleges in the state arrived to help. HA-You also became affiliated with and supported by Martin Luther King's Southern Christian Leadership Conference. Bitter white opposition ensued, in one instance in spring 1966, when the demonstrators sat on cement benches usually reserved for whites, a local judge ordered a group of white men to destroy the benches. They did so. One white graduate theology student from Southern Methodist University recalled making numerous trips from Dallas to Huntsville in order to achieve desegregation of public facilities in Huntsville. Ultimately the HA-You effort proved successful. Basically the city of Huntsville eliminated segregation of public accommodations by the end of the summer, 1966; full school desegregation, however, took until 1968.

Numerous other accomplishments can be accredited to Baker and the black and white anti-segregationists in Huntsville. What is important to remember is that not only were they struggling against segregation and anti-black behavior, they were attempting to dismantle an entire way of life and a culture of discrimination that permeated all levels of existence in Huntsville, as well as the remainder of Texas and the United States South. Baker and other blacks were elected to public office. As Bernadette Pruitt summarized: "the police department in the mid-1960s hired its first black officers since Reconstruction. The Texas Department of Criminal Justice also began hiring black correctional officers and secretarial staffers. The school system finally equalized teacher's salaries. African American clerical staff also worked in city and county offices."[4] The city of Huntsville and Walker County had undergone a cultural and political transformation. Wendell H. Baker Sr. deserves our praise for much of those accomplishments. He did not stop; he continued to involve himself in improving the lives of blacks and the rest of the community for the remainder of his life.[5]

In spite of Baker's remarkable life and successful career, little has been written about him. Contemporary scholars are recognizing his innumerable contributions. Sam Houston State University history professor, Bernadette Pruitt, authored an article entitled "Wendell Baker and the Civil Rights Movement in Huntsville, Texas."[6] Another SHSU historian, Jeff Littlejohn, was project director for the web-based site, "Democracy and Diversity in Walker County, Texas" of which Pruitt's work was a key part. Pruitt also is currently working on a book-length biography of Baker and his life. A brief internet piece by Cheval John refers to Baker as "The Martin Luther King of Huntsville." Retired Texas Southern University scholar, Naomi W. Ledé, included a section on Wendell Baker in her exhaustive study, *Samuel W. Houston and His Contemporaries*. Bernadette Pruitt and Naomi W. Ledé also wrote a biographical sketch of Baker for Ledé's *Pathfinders: A History of the Pioneering Efforts of African Americans, Huntsville, Walker County, Texas*.[7] Dan K. Utley and Milton S. Jordan reprinted a section from Baker's book, "Working the Polls on Election Day," in their collection, *Just Between Us: Stories and Memories from the Texas Pines*. Most recently, East Texas Historical Association director M. Scott Sosebee published a memorial on "Wendell Baker: Fighting for Rights for Sixty Years."[8]

In late summer, 2003, a few months before his 81st birthday, Wendell Baker sat down at his newly acquired computer and began to record his memories of a lifelong struggle for equality and justice for people of color. Nearly a year later Baker and a few friends and family published the first edition of *If Not Me, Who? What One Man Accomplished In His Battle for Equality*.[9]

Although, a few years later, some Sam Houston State University students had more copies printed, the book is now almost impossible to find. That was a significant factor in the editors' decision to reprint Baker's book. His book emphasizes the conditions within the black community that fit the patterns of other black civil rights activists in Texas and beyond. Baker's attempt to share his experiences mirrored the difficulties of other black writers. Baker could not locate a publisher, and self-published his book. Too many other Texas minority authors have struggled to have their books published and resorted either to not being able to have their works published, as did Afro-Texas novelist Lillian Jones Horace, *Angie Brown*, or self-publishing their works (which Horace also did for *Five Generations Hence*). So too did Naomi Ledé for her study, *Samuel W. Houston and His Contemporaries*.[10] Self-publishing usually meant that the book was not widely distributed, frequently remained unknown, and soon was out of print and difficult to locate. Neither of the co-editors of Baker's significant autobiography had been able to acquire a copy of his book. Fortunately, before he passed away, Baker loaned his only copy to us from which to make a Xerox copy. We made a copy and returned the book to Wendell H. Baker, Sr.

With the permission of Wendell Baker, his help, and that of his friends and family, we have produced this new edition with notes and comment. Our hope is to make this significant record of the struggle for equality in East Texas more readily available for historians, researchers and other interested readers. *If Not Me, Who?* points out what one person with the help and support of others can accomplish. It is an instructive memoir of the struggle in one small East Texas city that reflects similar experiences across the South.

Wendell Baker's recollections cover the decades from before World War II into the 21st century. His memories of the more intense struggles are focused on the mid-20th century when public school integration, freedom rides, lunch counter sit ins and marches in Washington D.C., Selma, Alabama, and elsewhere were regularly in the news. These were years when violence, often deadly violence, was a reality for those who dared challenge a pervasive system of racial discrimination. Baker and his companions in Huntsville and Walker County joined this challenge in the face of white resistance and of this very real threat of violence.

His book is not a history of the civil rights struggle in Walker County, Texas. It is the recollection, 30 to 40 years and more removed, of an intelligent and determined man directly involved in those struggles. Those who lived and acted during those years will have memories of their own involvement. Baker's memories make clear that he and his companions are responsible for much of the progress that grew out of those struggles. His book reminds us of the importance of hearing minority voices and of the difficulty minority writers had and continue to have in getting their work into print.

We have included a few notes to put these events in their time period and to make clear the identity of some of the people and places mentioned. We have included a portion of Dr. Naomi W. Lede's book, *Samuel W. Houston and His Contemporaries*, that was included, with permission, in Baker's original edition. We also included a section from former Republican political leader (Secretary of the Treasury and Secretary of State) James A. Baker's memoir, *Work Hard, Study . . .and Keep Out of Politics*.[11] The latter is included under the title "Discovering an Extended Family" and is used with permission. These two brief narratives provide helpful information about Wendell Baker's life and his extended family. We have added to the Index and Bibliography that were part of Baker's original autobiography. Referred to as the "Jackie Robinson of the Golden Triangle," the "Martin Luther King of Huntsville and Walker County," and a colleague and relative of other accomplished individuals such as Dan Rather and James Baker, Wendell Baker left a legacy of commitment and action on behalf of making life better for the people of Texas and beyond. That legacy deserves much wider recognition.

Credit: From WORK HARD, STUDY...AND KEEP OUT OF POLITICS! by James A. Baker III, with Steve Fiffer, copyright (c) 2006 by James A. Baker III. Used by permission of G. P. Putnam's Sons, a division of Penguin Group (USA) LLC

Notes

1. Wendell Baker, *If Not Me, Who? What One Man Accomplished In His Battle For Equality* (Huntsville, Texas: privately printed, 2004), 33.
2. Baker, *If Not Me Who?*, 16.
3. Bernadette Pruitt, "Wendell Baker and the Civil Rights Movement in Huntsville, Texas" (http://www.studythepast.com/democracy/wendell_baker_home.htm), 5.
4. Pruitt, "Wendell Baker and the Civil Rights Movement in Huntsville, Texas," 7.
5. Much more information on this critical aspect of Baker's life can be found in his autobiography and in the biographical section written by Dr. Naomi W. Ledé.
6. Pruitt, "Wendell Baker and the Civil Rights Movement in Huntsville, Texas."
7. Jeff Littlejohn, "Democracy and Diversity in Walker County, Texas" (http://www.studythepast.com/democracy/personnel.htm); Cheval John, "Wendell Baker: The Martin Luther King of Huntsville" (http://vallanomedia.com/2011/02/01/wendell-baker); Naomi W. Lede, *Samuel W. Houston and His Contemporaries* (Houston: Pha Green Printing, 1981); Bernadette Pruitt and Naomi W. Ledé, "Wendell H. Baker, Sr.," in *Pathfinders: A History of the Pioneering Efforts of African Americans, Huntsville, Walker County, Texas*, edited by Naomi W. Ledé (Virginia Beach, Virginia: Donning Company Publishers, 2004), 155-157.
8. Wendell Baker, "Working the Polls on Election Day," in *Just Between Us: Stories and Memories from the Texas Pines*, edited by Dan K. Utley and Milton S. Jordan (Nacogdoches, Tex.: Stephen F. Austin State University Press, 2012), 125-126; Scott Sosebee, "Wendell Baker: Fighting for Rights for Sixty Years," *The Daily Sentinel* (Nacogdoches), November 24, 2013.
9. Baker, *If Not Me Who?*
10. Lillian Jones Horace novel, *Angie Brown*, would not be published until rescued in 2008 by Texas Southern scholar Karen Kossie-Chernyshev. Lillian Jones Horace, *Five Generations Hence*, in *Recovering Five Generations Hence: The Life and Writings of Lillian Jones Horace*, edited by Karen Kossie-Chernyshev (College Station: Texas A&M University Press, 2013); Ledé, *Samuel W. Houston and His Contemporaries*.
11. James A. Baker, III with Steve Fiffer, *"Work Hard, Study . . . and Keep Out of Politics": Adventures and Lessons from an Unexpected Public Life* (New York: G. P. Putnam's Sons, 2006).

If Not Me, Who?

What One Man Accomplished In His Battle For Equality

Wendell Baker

PREFACE

The assistance I have received in getting this material ready for publishing has been superb, and the encouragement, along with the help, has been most rewarding. I had no computer skills and made it known, but that was not an acceptable excuse since so many friendly, knowledgeable people offered their assistance; Cynthia Willis and Iantha Ross with their superb typing skills; my grandson, Justin Harrison and Dr. Bernadette Pruitt of the History Department of Sam Houston State University; Dr Bernice Strauss, Mrs. Margorie Oliphant-Bennett who was one of my former high school students and now a retired public school teacher; Dr. Naomi Lede, author of "Samuel Walker Houston and his Contemporaries"; Dr. Gary Zellar, whose master's thesis on, "History of Huntsville Public Schools," provided so much research data that was important for my "latent memory" of so many details of some events.

Going through life might easily be compared to a walk through the forest passing the objects that might deflect your route without paying noticeable attention to what they might have done to add miles on your trip toward your destiny. These obstacles might have been a tree, or a limb, or a berry-vine with stickers or simply an ant hill in your path, but one chose simply to go around it without notice or thought. So at the end of your journey you have simply forgotten what you saw but you did change your path and directions a bit, not remembering why.

So it was with me until a friend of mine, Scott Plummer,[1] called me to his house, and said, "What are you doing? Come down to my house. I want to show you something". We walked to his office door, and he pointed to a computer on his desk and said, "That is for you, and all I ask is that you write a book about your life". I was pleasantly shocked, but I did seriously consider his offer. That's when I began to try seriously to "remember" what I had passed and barely noticed. Then I realized that many of the incidences I barely remembered if at all. Isn't this the way we all do it? Now I realize that the human mind can perceive but not always record details of events that result in one's destiny. Therefore, this book reflects the recollections of this journey "in part," that changed drastically the journey, and the future for myself and others.

Chapter One

FAMILY BACKGROUND

I think I was born to be an activist. My father, Jesse Baker, had only a fourth grade education and my mother, Fannie Willis Baker had but a seventh grade education available to her. Despite this, they knew how important an education would be for their children.

On November 13, 1922, I was born the eighth of ten children. They named me Wendell Harold. My earliest memory is of an approximately 100-acre farm they owned about eight miles, west of Huntsville, Texas out in the "boonies" of Walker County.

I vaguely remember our house, built on a hillside with an "L" shaped porch, which was high off the ground. The hill sloped down toward a "branch" or "gully", depending on whether it was the wet or dry season. Across the gully lived one of our tenant families, a young couple also with a large family, who helped us farm our land.

It was difficult for black children to go to school, but my parents wanted their children to have an opportunity for a high school education. With this in mind, in the fall of my second year, my dad bought another farm closer to town and we made the move from the Cotton Creek Community into the Pine Hill Community.[2]

The older boys and some of our tenants helped my dad move our possessions into the new house, then sent back for the rest of the family. It was an old house, but new to us and much larger with an upstairs and two fireplaces. Even then my father had to add an addition to provide adequate space for all of his children to sleep and play comfortably (or as comfortable as we could be in this time period). My dad was an industrious man who ventured out to make things happen for his family, such as the major accomplishment of purchasing a home and seeing to it that we paid cash for most of what we acquired.

Chapter Two

FAMILY EXPANSION AND COMMUNIY RELATIONSHIPS

We cleared more land around our new house, which had a live flowing spring creek and very fertile black bottom land. This rich soil grew various crops including corn, cotton and sugar cane with little or no fertilizer. I remember, as a very small child picking peas and cotton with my older brothers and sisters. The land near the creek produced wild okra in abundance, which my mother prepared in many delicious ways.

We raised hay for the horses and mules, which were our source of power to do the farming. Dad also raised cattle, some so gentle that they were a source of milk for the family. He supplied local markets with beef and pork, which we had raised.

Our family had ample food, which we shared with the community, for having a sufficient food supply was rare in those times. We knew how to preserve food and also planted crops adaptable to cold weather. We were continually building additional houses to accommodate more tenants who helped us farm. Tenants were defined as individuals who had no place to live or resources of their own with which to farm and make a living, for farming was the main enterprise of that era. Many of the people looked for someone to live with who had land and domestic animals to supply their basic needs. We eventually had five tenant houses and families living on our land and we stayed at this capacity for many years.

There were many large families in the community who had boys and no jobs for them so my father would hire them to help with breaking and preparing the land for planting and harvesting the crops. All of this heavy manual labor was done by hand. My dad had a tent and the young men would live there throughout the year, or as long as the weather was tolerable. During the cold winter days we would bring them inside until it was warmer.

Many times my brothers and I would choose to stay in the tent with them because we considered it to be fun. Sometimes the young men would prefer to sleep in the barn on the hay or on the cotton in the cotton house.

My mother and sisters along with the help of the boys would prepare the meals for all the workers. In this way all of the Baker boys learned how to cook. Our dining table could accommodate from 12 to 18 people at one time. Many times we would serve the first set, then clean the dining table, reset it, and start again to serve the next set. This went on until all were fed. We always served family style so everyone could get enough food.

We served as a source of revenue for many families in the area for my father had jobs for everyone as not only did he have crops and cattle but he owned both a sawmill and a pulpwood and logging business. When school was out in the summer he would send his truck to town and pick up everyone, including children and prisoners, who wanted to work, regardless of race or creed. Many intelligent young men, who were able to do a variety of jobs with skill and efficiency, lacked a formal education due to their economic situations. Jobs were scarce, and the only work available was on farms.

The United States was struggling, which made conditions extremely difficult for young Black men and their families. Living with us was one of the best situations these young men had ever experienced, so many stayed on from year to year, some until they became adults and married. As an example of how scarce jobs were and how eager young people were to make a living and establish financial stability for themselves, there was an event concerning Uncle Frank Willis, who lived in LaMarque, Texas and worked at the "Waterfront", (sometimes called "the wharf") in Galveston. He drove daily from LaMarque to Galveston. For he was one of the few men who had a good "public job"(as it was called in those days), and on the weekends when he wasn't working he would "hang out" at the corner store with friends. He mentioned having a brother-in-law, (my father, Jesse Baker), who owned a farm and how many young men stayed with us and worked on the farm. He was unaware anyone had a particular interest in farm work, but one of the young men listening became very interested. This young man had no job and had no prospects so he decided to walk from LaMarque to Huntsville, a distance of more than 100 miles. It took him about a week as he started from LaMarque begging for food along the way. He traveled through the City of Houston and up Highway 75 to Huntsville. When he reached Huntsville he asked people if they knew Jesse Baker, the man my uncle had been talking about. He was immediately directed to where my family lived. He came out to our farm, met my dad and family and told us about his trip and why he came. He described his travels in detail and I remember my family listening to him with amazement. Of course my dad hired him immediately and he lived with us for many years and became like a brother in our family. About fifteen years later, he decided to go back to try and find his family.

Another young man from the community, A. C. Harris, also lived with us even though his large family lived nearby.[3] A. C. later became one of the most highly respected ministers in Huntsville. As A. C. tells it, when he told my father he wanted to become a minister my father took him to the local bank and told the President of the bank to let him have whatever money he needed to get started. I was reared in an environment where sharing and respecting others cultivated self-reliance.

As a little boy, I started working in the fields with my elders and continued on through my high school years. When I finished high school at the age of 16, I had not worked for anyone outside of our own family operations. Going through school was one of the requirements of my mother and father, for if we did not desire an education we could no longer live at home. Those who didn't finish high school and were old enough to work and live on their own moved on to other places but I chose to stay in school. Many days we would walk from where we lived into town to school. We didn't get a weather forecast in those days, so frequently in the morning it would be a beautiful day with everyone warm and comfortable. But sometimes it would start raining later in the day and by evening when we were ready to leave school, we would get what we called a "blue norther" where temperatures could drop 20 to 30 degrees and we would become chilled to the bone without enough clothing. Frequently, when the weather was terrible, we had to walk home from school.

Many families along the way knew us well for they had come to the farm and assisted in picking and chopping cotton. When they saw us walking past their homes in the cold or rain they invited us in to warm up and sent the older boys on ahead to bring back horses. Three or four of the children walking home would get on one horse and would ride home together. Families worked for, and with, one another, for our community was a large extended family.

When we were 11 or 12 years old we would still walk to school barefooted, because it was not considered unusual. Today, it would be embarrassing to see children attending school without shoes, but during my childhood it was no problem. Many children even went to high school without shoes due to a lack of finances.

Wendell and Augusta Baker in 1943, before their marriage.
Photo courtesy of the Baker family

Chapter Three

EARLY SCHOOL EXPERIENCES AND LIMITATIONS AND COLLEGE EXPERIENCES

School was an interesting time in my life. With no school buses, many children waited until another child in the family was of age before attending school, for this meant two or more could walk together. During my elementary school years, many in my class had sisters or brothers who were in the same grade but different ages. For example, Grover and his sister, the two Archie sisters,[4] the Ferguson sisters, as well as my sister Nannie Lee and I were all in the same class. Despite this arrangement, the class was not large due to many families not allowing their children to walk so far to attend school at such a young age for many of the parents believed it was too far for the children to walk. Almost none of our tenant families' children attended school, but instead they played or hunted. The children in my family, however, had to attend school and we soon learned to accept it and enjoy it as this became the norm. Owning the farm provided my family with other advantages such as owning an automobile, which occasionally meant transportation to and from school.

In later years my dad would frequently take us to school and pick us up. But this made little difference in our lifestyle. Every morning, on school days, the alarm clock went off at 4:00 a. m. and every one of school age began the day with daily chores before going to school.

Many times in winter we would walk to school because the roads were so muddy and bad. We would leave before daylight, but we knew our way in the dark and were well on our way by sunrise.

When I was about 8 or 9 years of age my aunt Hattie Williams wanted me to come and live with her in Galveston. While there I attended the West District Elementary School and also the Avenue L Baptist Church. At this time the school district began building a new school building. My Aunt Hattie was a talented seamstress, and well known in the community. Her business as a seamstress became so lucrative that she was able to employ two young ladies to assist her.

I spent two years in Galveston but became homesick, and, as I missed my family, I decided to rejoin my brothers and sisters at the farm. Happy and excited to see them, I reconnected to my family of ten and continued an ever developing bond that I appreciate to this day.

I started attending school again in Huntsville and discovered the books issued in the Huntsville school that year were the exact ones I had while in Galveston. After discussing this with my teacher and principal, Samuel Walker Houston, I was placed in a higher grade alongside of my sister, Nannie Lee.

The books we were issued had been used for several years by White students and were missing many pages. Despite this we managed to use them as "best we could" and I graduated with my class with honors.

My high school class was represented by families from Walker, Trinity, San Jacinto, Grimes, Madison, Leon and Montgomery counties, for Huntsville was one of the first towns between Beaumont and Austin, (east and west) and Houston and Dallas (north and south) with a high school for Blacks. Samuel Walker Houston had founded this private high school west of Huntsville in the Galilee community.

Colleges in the area available to Blacks included Mary Allen College in Crockett, Prairie View A & M near Hempstead, Paul Quinn College in Waco, Bishop College and Wiley College in Marshall, Samuel Huston College and Tillotson College in Austin, Texas College in Tyler and Jarvis College in Hawkins, Texas. Each of these colleges offered courses for students to complete their high school requirements, with options for college credits.

We did not have many students in school, as the average class size was only 30 to 40 students with even less in the elementary school, because as stated, there weren't many young children whose parents were sending them to school. The students who were in my high school were seriously interested in an education and worked hard to succeed. Many of them went on to college. Just the idea of even getting a college education was extremely important at that time.

We had a prestigious band consisting of perhaps fifteen students whose parents could afford to buy them an instrument. We didn't go out on the field and perform like they do today, but just sat in the stands and played the three or four tunes we knew. It was also an honor to be in the choral group, led by Mrs. Florence Glenn Chritien, who was an excellent pianist, as well as an inspirational teacher. She excelled in choral music and could pick up any tune that was hummed to her and play it back as though she was reading the music, Mason Steele Frazier, our science teacher, was another accomplished pianist.

By my senior year, our band instructor, Bradley Moore, had moved to Palestine, Texas to teach at their high school. This required Professor Samuel Walker Houston to hire someone to keep the band going, and see to it that we always had a pianist to play for our school functions and commencement exercises. By my senior year I became a tenor singer in the choral group and could also play most of the band instruments.

After finishing high school, I was unable to enter college immediately, so in the fall of that year I got my first job working at Sam Houston State Teacher's College preparing meals for the students at Belvin Hall. My salary was only twenty dollars a month and I started working at 6 a. m. each morning. We would prepare and serve breakfast, clean up, prepare and serve lunch and clean up again. If I got finished by 2 p.m. I could take off for a couple of hours to go down to the high school campus to spend my free time with the students in an attempt to keep the band going. There still was no band teacher, so I worked with the students and taught the new band members about the instruments. In this manner I learned how to play every instrument in the band including the trombone, saxophone, bass tuba, and piano.

I worked at Belvin Hall for five months and managed to save forty dollars. I started there in late summer after I graduated from high school and worked until the end of January. While working at the college I was invited to take a trip with a group of students from the high school to visit Samuel Huston College campus where my former science teacher, Mason Steele Frazier's father was on the faculty. Mason was extremely impressed with me for two reasons. I spent many hours in the science lab and I was a farm boy who had been reared butchering calves, hogs, Squirrels and rabbits for food.

In the science department I became an expert at stuffing frogs and lizards. To do taxidermy, the body is taken out through the mouth of the animal with strong tongs. The skin is then turned inside out to remove all of the meat. The skin is dried and the body is stuffed with clay and molded back into shape. The eyes are simulated with artificial eyes or buttons. I got to be such an expert with these small animals that I began thinking that I wanted to become a doctor. On this trip to Samuel Huston College, I discovered Mr. Frazier had taken many of my stuffed animals to his college friends. Almost every office had one or more of my stuffed animals on display as paperweights. The faculty was not only impressed to find that I had taxidermy skills but more importantly that I could play almost every instrument in the band. Because of this I received a scholarship to Samuel Huston College where I played in their orchestra, which also served as their dance band.

This was the era of big bands and the Samuel Huston college orchestra was comprised of fifteen to twenty excellent young musicians. We played for high school proms in different cities and many of the students for whom we played were so impressed that they in turn enrolled in Samuel Huston College.

The college also had one of the best a cappella choirs in the southwest because of R. Nathaniel Dett,[5] one of the world's foremost composers and arrangers who had been there. He was supposed to have been on the faculty at Samuel Huston College, but he was called a lecturer because he was really doing most of his work at the University of Texas where he was getting paid. The University of Texas was able to use him because of his title as a lecturer. I regret not getting to work with him but he was there before my time.

Though the music scholarship was primarily what helped me attend college and we were one of the best dance bands in the area, I soon discovered that most of the band members cared little about their college scholarship and what it meant. We were very popular, playing for dances, proms and night clubs in cities like Dallas, San Antonio, Waco and Austin but many times, after being up all night, we didn't feel like being in classes the next day. I tried a few of these "gigs", as we called them, and discovered it was definitely not what I wanted to do.

I wanted to stay in school so I left the band and began singing in the choir. They had an eighty-voice choir that traveled around entertaining at churches and big events, which proved to be a marvelous asset to the school and its excellent music department. I started singing with the choir during my first full year in college as an advanced freshman, and was chosen from that group of eighty voices to be the tenor singer in a sextet. That year we traveled to California and toured the Southern California Methodist Conference to raise money to support our college. This was before the days of The United Negro College Fund. We sang for every major church in the Methodist Conference of Southern California, which extended from San Diego to Los Angeles. Those two cities alone took up all of our time because they were so extensive. Frequently we sang for radio stations that belonged to Bob Hope and Bing Crosby and I had the privilege of meeting them. I also met Jackie Robinson, who was then a college student in the Los Angeles area. Hope and Crosby made substantial contributions to our school, as did Helms Bakery. We sang for the Helms workers and they absolutely loved our music.

One of the reasons why my years at Samuel Huston College were exciting was because of the interesting people I met. One of the young men who sang in the sextet with me, Maceo Pembroke eventually became a very popular minister, who some years later collaborated on a book of traditional spirituals and other songs.[6] Those were wonderful years at Samuel Huston College, but far too short.

Chapter Four

COLLEGE, FARM DEFERMENT, MARRIAGE ARMY INDUCTION AND TRAINING

My college days came to a screeching halt when the war broke out. I had gone home on a trip with some students who were visiting Prairie View College and while I was home Japan bombed Pearl Harbor. I knew immediately what a momentous event it was because I had seen a movie explaining the Navy operations there. My dad had just bought a new car and he was taking me back to the Prairie View campus when we learned of the bombing on the car radio while on the highway. Following the bombing, President Franklin D. Roosevelt and Congress announced a declaration of war. I was old enough to have registered for the army so when I returned home again for the Christmas holidays I received my induction papers. I already had two brothers in the service; James was in the navy and Herbert was in the Army Medical Corps, so my dad immediately started procedures to get me deferred. He was successful in having me reclassified 3C, a farm deferment. I had to notify the college authorities that I would not be able to come back to school because it was necessary for me to be engaged full-time in farming. My dad had expanded and now owned a tractor and a couple of trucks for the farm. When I returned home and took charge of the farming operations I found that I was very capable and we were able to greatly expand our beef, hog, and egg production. We also began producing lumber and timber products for paper. These many varied enterprises kept me busy for the next two years but eventually I was inducted into the U. S. Army.[7]

I met an attractive "little lady" while I was on the farm deferment, who was living in Houston with an aunt while attending school. When I was inducted into the military I was originally sent to Fort Sam Houston, then to Fort Lewis Washington for basic training, and later to Camp Crowder Missouri for my technical assignment. It was at Camp Crowder that I got married, for that attractive "little lady", Augusta Lee, had agreed to become Augusta Lee Baker.[8]

When I was sent back to Fort Sam Houston in San Antonio, Texas for my technical training as a surgical technician in the Medical Corps, Augusta told me that she would write me a letter every day while I was in service and she did. Sometimes when we were moved to another camp, several days would pass before the mail caught up with us. When we answered mail call, the mail clerk would call each soldier's name. There were times when the mail clerk would stop calling names and just throw me the mailbag.

When we finally reached Japan and got settled down in concrete warehouses where we were to live, another soldier, Ebenezer Bush, and I were assigned to a port dispensary for duty as medical personnel. Bush was a graduate of Tuskegee University in the field of Chemistry and had taken many of his courses under Doctor George Washington Carver, who was on the faculty at Tuskegee. I was assigned to Medical Administrative work while Bush was assigned to the Laboratory. We were the only two Blacks in this medical unit, for the Armed Services were not integrated at that time. When we arrived, there were about 30 service men working in this port dispensary including three physicians.

Since the fighting was over and many ship loads of men and equipment were still coming in, many of our coworkers were eligible to go back to the States. As they left to go home new soldiers were assigned to work with us. In this group, we had master sergeants, first sergeants, technical sergeants, staff sergeants, corporals, privates first class, and the lowest, just privates. As these young men came in, they assumed the titles and promotions of those leaving, but somehow Bush and I never got these promotions. They were never offered to us. Although most of these young White men coming into the unit had no college training and Bush had a Bachelor's Degree and I was a college junior. The newcomers were given the rank and drew the salaries while Bush and I were given the difficult assignments and the responsibility of supervising the performance and further training of the new personnel. Very soon, with the exchange of personnel, Bush was head of the Laboratory and I headed the administrative services and immunization teams (four teams of five men each). The young men working for us were cooperative and respectful because the physicians under whom we worked would not have had it any other way. The reasons given the two of us for not getting promotions was that the port dispensary of the Army Medical Corps was not authorized to have any minority personnel and the trucking company, where we were assigned for rations and quarters, was not authorized any medical personnel. We considered ourselves caught between the devil and the deep blue sea.

When it came our time to return to the states, we were offered various incentives to re-enlist in the Armed Services. My answer was, "Hell no, I am going home"! But, when I got home I found everything was just as I had left it. Racism, Hate, Intolerance and Bigotry. (These words are capitalized for a reason.)

Chapter Five

RETURN FROM SERVICE IN JAPAN
COMPLETION OF COLLEGE
FIRST JOB: TEACHING HIGH SHOOL

After we got off the ship and again on the train returning to Fort Sam Houston, the "N" word, was constantly being used in our presence by our White comrades. This was disappointing and demeaning. We had come back to a segregated society that was called a "democracy" with hostile anti-black leadership, poor schools, and no provisions in the state for higher education. Hate and racism were still the law-of- the- land, sanctioned, supported and enforced by the elected officials and a legal system that we had pledged our lives to defend. I considered this to be one hell of a note. Now, I found that I was lost again and what was I to do?

The University of Texas was sued by Heman Marion Sweatt who wanted to attend the Law School, so the State of Texas built a so-called "separate but equal" facility in Houston called the Texas State University for Negroes. From this so-called "equal facility", I was the first to graduate with a degree in Chemistry[9] (The following year the name of the University was changed to Texas Southern University.) But because I was unable financially to go to medical school and Texas had no provisions for Blacks to enter higher professions, I settled for teaching science at the high school level in Huntsville, Texas.

I was hired by chance when I was home from college for a short visit. I was walking down the street in the shopping area of Huntsville. Standing in front of a dry goods store was the man who had given me the job at Sam Houston State College some years before. Ottie Barrett no longer worked for the college and was now in the dry goods business. I stopped and spoke to him and he asked me what I was doing. I informed him that in a few weeks I would be graduating from college with a Bachelor's degree in Chemistry. He said that if I wanted to teach he had a position for me. He was a member of the school board at that time, and told me to come back to his office in about two hours, at which time he had the superintendent of schools with him. They told me that I was just the man that they wanted and asked if I would teach the sciences for them. I agreed to do so.

I came back to Samuel Walker Houston High School to head a science department that had absolutely no science equipment at all. I was to teach General Science to ninth graders, Biology to tenth graders, Chemistry to eleventh graders and Physics to twelfth grade girls only. The twelfth grade boys did not take Physics because they were required to take Woodworking in the shop. There was no equipment for teaching the sciences, no chemical balances, no burners, no microscopes, no chemical tables and no running water. I mean absolutely nothing!

In my first week of school I made it my business to meet the White science teacher from the White high school and he invited me to look at his science lab for teaching. It was not the best, but it was far more than what I had. We went into his storeroom and there were shelves of microscopes, burners, flasks, chemical balances, etc. I backed my car up to the curb and opened the trunk and we started loading. When I finished, I told him to take those items off his inventory because I did not intend to bring them back. By this method, I secured a little of the basic equipment. The students at Samuel Walker Houston had never even seen a microscope, a Bunsen burner or a chemical balance, nothing at all. All would be new to them.

The ninth grade class was divided into two sections of about 50 students each. The tenth grade biology class had 118 students. We couldn't even get all the students inside the door. The students with the best behavior were allowed to sit outside against the wall. It was a terrible situation that really was never improved.

After the Supreme Court decision in 1954 on integration, Huntsville built a new high school. Yet for the first year I did not even have a blackboard in my classroom. Despite this, each year my chemistry students would score high enough that they were able to enter the National Science Foundation summer school program. I was told by a college professor who did research in this area for a book that was being written that more of my students went on to become medical doctors, dentists, nurses, chemists, high school science-teachers, physicists and specialists in other science related fields than ever before.

While teaching, I started working as a broadcaster at a radio station and for eight years did seven shows per week known as the "Bronze Variety Hour". Dan Rather, the CBS news anchor, was working along with me when he was a student at Sam Houston State University. We broadcasted many of the programs and football games together.[10]

I also worked with the agriculture department at Sam Houston High School to help boys develop their talents for the New Farmers of America farm club. This organization was to the Black agriculture program what the Future Farmers of America was to the White students. While teaching, I also developed seven quartets that went to the National Competition in Atlanta, Georgia. Five of these quartets won first place and two quartets won second place on the national level. To qualify, they had to win their district, bi-district, state, and finally their area, which was composed of, Oklahoma, Arkansas, Texas, and Louisiana. The first quartet included Calvin Smith, Jimmy Franklin, and the two others. Other quartets were composed of Earl

Murray, William Baines, and Sammy Smith and another name that I also can't recall, followed by Bobby Merchant, T. L. Toliver, John Henry Glaze, and John Williams. Also James Earl Harrison, Howard Rogers, Waydell Maxey and Billy Ray Jones formed a quartet, as did George McGowan, Lynn Jones and two others. My last quartet consisted of Anthony (Jack) Branch, Paul Jones, Joe Teamer, and Tommy Young, three of those members still sing together[11] Two became ministers and the third is a retired educator. This quartet recorded an album entitled, "My Mother's Favorite Hymns".

All these students were average or above in their scholastic work for I refused to work with trying to develop a student who did not apply himself. Several of them were honor students and had excellent attendance and behavioral records, which made them a pleasure to work with.

I also enjoyed my science classes and would often take my students on field trips so they could experience learning situations that could not be brought to the classroom. For these field trips the students needed money to pay for the buses we used, but their caring parents, even though they were poor, always found a way to support these projects for their children.

One time we were studying about how large bodies of water and mountains would affect weather and climate conditions. Many of these students had never seen a mountain or the desert so we took a trip to West Texas. We left on a Friday night so we could be in the area by daylight. I had the class president and secretary write to the mayor and Chamber of Commerce of the towns where we would spend time. Whenever we reached our destination the people were always expecting us and were very cordial.

On one of our trips though, as we were returning home in order to be back for Sunday morning, we encountered blatant race prejudice in Austin, Texas. I had always informed my students that when we stopped at a service station for fuel, to expect the same service that anyone else would receive.

We had three buses that held about 100 gallons of gasoline or more when empty. And as we knew we would be traveling all night with no other service stations open on the route we would take, we needed to stop and fill up. Since I had my students understand my acceptable conduct, they adhered and understood though they called me, "mean and strict". When we pulled into a service station in Austin, Texas the students got out to use the facilities. The service station operator immediately attempted to stop them. But I stopped him instead and said, "If my students can't use your rest room, we cannot use your products". Then I walked across the street to another station and told them what had happen, they invited us over to their station. I returned and told our bus drivers to drive across the street. The students also bought everything that station had to eat; we serviced our buses and returned home. Those students never forgot that lesson and for weeks following this experience we took part of our science class period to discuss such events.

On a trip to the airport in Houston we went aboard the huge passenger planes, even into the cockpits and then into the radio towers to watch the air traffic controllers direct the planes. We also visited The Battleship Texas near Houston. They particularly enjoyed this because it was the first time they had seen a very large ship made of steel floating like a fish. When we observed San Jacinto Battle ground tower, I had them stand and look up at the tower and watch it waive back and forth but not fall. I didn't explain this before going there because I wanted to "catch" these students after we were back in class. Upon our return, I asked them to tell me why that tower was rocking back and forth and I received many answers and arguments from the students, it was fun. Of course the tower was not moving. As they attempted to stand very still to look up at the tower their bodies were moving and not the tower.

After teaching for twelve years, trying tactfully to develop my student's thinking and reasoning abilities, I was terminated from the position. I will not call it "my job", because my dad taught us that a job belongs to the person who gave it to you and he defined a job as, "something that someone cannot do or does not want to do, and as a result, someone else is compensated to do it". The compensation for doing a job is "the least that one will pay for the quality and quantity one is expecting". If someone else's time and service can be acquired for less than you are getting, you no longer have, "a job". Sometimes one is asked to surrender his manhood, freedom, pride, and even his material belongings in order to hold a job. This happened to me.

I decided to build a home for my wife and three children, which I considered my greatest assets.[12] I wanted to take advantage of the things that had been promised to us as Veterans and live as well as possible. First I went to the bank where my dad had opened a bank account for me when I was a 16 year old and just out of high school. I talked to the bank president and told him I wanted a loan to build a house with the government guarantee, as promised when we were discharged from the armed services. His answer was, "We cannot do that". The Veterans administrations would finance a home for Veterans with a guarantee of up to eighty or ninety percent to the lender at a given interest rate. I was refused by the lending institutions in Huntsville, so I went to Houston to a loan shark type of operation that agreed at a high interest rate. I designed my home, had blue prints drawn up by a professional, and went back to my Huntsville bank for an interim loan. The banker again refused me so I went back to the same Loan Shark in Houston and got a letter of commitment saying that they would buy the note or pay for the house if built to my plans and specifications. The local banker told me he would not lend me the money to build this house but he would make a loan to Mr. V. C., a White man, to build this house for me. I refused to accept that.

I took my plans to the city lumber company, owned by Clyde Hall,[13] who was on the school board and he agreed to furnish the materials for my project if I would assign him the right to finish in case I would or could not do so. That implied that, if I defaulted, he would have the building completed and get his investment back and could sell it. I agreed.

I started with my building program in late October of 1960 with the help of my brother-in-law, Woodrow Wilson, a Houston builder. He agreed to give up his work in Houston and help me get my house started. I was building on property that I had purchased from my older brother, Claude, and which bordered on what is now FM 1374. At that time it was just a simple county dirt road. While building my home, a contractor was hired to construct a man-made lake down the road beyond my place. This beautiful lake was built to accommodate the "white elite" with lake front homes.

As my building program progressed, suspicion and animosity arose. Every evening there was a parade of cars and pickup trucks along the road in front of my home. I had not cleared out all the trees and undergrowth that obstructed the view from the road, so in order to see better, many of the sightseers just parked on the side of the road and sat and stared. This happened daily, particularly in the late afternoons, after the businesses in town had closed. There was only about a "city block" length on the road from which one could get a good view but on Sundays after church services, sometimes more than twenty cars could be seen along this open stretch. Many times people would get out of their cars and stand beside them. Others would leave their cars to join a group from other cars and they would just stand and talk. Seldom did anyone come down to the structure where we were working. For the several months I was building I seldom saw any Blacks among the spectators.

On weekends I hired high school boys to come and help me. They enjoyed making a little money and I fed them well. By the end of the Christmas holiday season, the house-building project was far enough along that I was able to move my family in. The crowd began to lessen, but on Sundays there would still be 10 to 20 cars out on the public dirt road.

The Black teachers in the Huntsville Independent School District only got 1-year contracts, at the state minimal salary scale. After 12 years in the system my monthly check was still below three hundred dollars. Our principal told the Black teachers, "You do not need more than a one year contract". "You are already overpaid". The new contracts were sent to teachers by the principal around the middle of April, but that year I was not awarded a contract. Other teachers received theirs, but I was not included.

Finally, our new principal, met me in the hallway and said, "Mr. Baker, the superintendent did not send your contract and said he would like to talk with you.[14] Go over and see him now. I will get someone to keep your classroom, and if you come up to my office I will call him and tell him you are coming." I agreed. I drove down to the Superintendent's office, and when I walked in the door he did not greet me. He merely said, "Wendell, if you will sell that house you got out there, that's causing so much controversy with the White folks, I'll give you your contract".

I said, "It is not for sale. I built it myself for my family". The Superintendent then said, "Just go on back to the school. I can't help you. This is your last year here with us". I went back to my classroom and finished the month ahead of me. This ended my teaching career.[15]

I had acquired a farm tractor, hay baler and other equipment. Some days I would make as much bailing hay with the use of my equipment as I had earned in a month as a teacher. However, I was still a radio announcer with seven shows a week but before long the "powers that be" had me removed from this position also. Anyway, we survived.

One day I stopped by the County Agents office. He had just received a letter from an employment agency in Houston wanting "rural reared" young Black men to apply with them for work. There was a petro-chemical plant coming into the area that was interested in hiring them. One of the young men in the County Agents office was trying to get a ride to Houston, and as I was going to Houston myself within an hour, I told him he could ride with me.

When we arrived I took care of my business and then drove him to the address where he could apply. It was a hot day, and I did not wish to wait in the car, so I went inside with him. It was during the lunch hour and the receptionist told us her boss was not but would return soon. She gave both of us a cold drink and asked us to wait for him. After nearly thirty minutes she saw we were getting restless so she brought us some test papers and said, "I know my boss would want you to take this, so if you do not mind, I will let you proceed with this test". We had a given number of minutes to complete the test and when we finished, she took the papers to another room. In a few minutes she returned, told us her boss still had not returned and gave us a second test that we also finished in the time allotted. She again took the papers and disappeared. Each time she gave us the test papers she told us how many minutes we had to complete the tests. Finally, she brought in a test and said we could take as long as we wished to complete it.

Since I had received training in testing and measurements in college, I recognized these tests and the method in which they were given. The first test was a general aptitude test, the second was for mechanical aptitude, and the third was a personality test. The receptionist graded all the tests and asked us to wait for the manager. The manager arrived, introduced himself and asked me to come upstairs and talk with him. He wanted to know where I had taken my mechanical training. I told him I had been a farm boy had taught myself in order to keep the old equipment running. Also, I had been a high school science teacher for twelve years and had taught my students the same principles on which I was tested. I did not tell him I had administered many such tests myself, graded them and done the profiles on hundreds of students. This standardized testing program was supposed to be the job of the counselor in our high school, but because of my special training, it fell to my lot.

The manager said he would be submitting this information to a petro-chemical company and if I did not hear from them within five days I should call him. He assured me he would have something for me. He also told me that I had made the highest score on the mechanical aptitude test in all his testing.

In a few days I received a telephone call from the Goodyear Tire and Rubber Company Chemical Plant in Beaumont, Texas and I was asked to come down and talk with them.[16] Robert Cliborne, head of the Quality Control Division, interviewed me and concluded with, "Would you come and work for me"? I promised I would. Mr. Cliborne informed me that he was not able to tell me what my salary would be at the time, but that he would meet with the plant council and they would determine what my salary would be and he would send me a letter of confirmation. I received the letter with an offer and a request that I not divulge the amount of my salary to any of my co-workers. He said, "You will be bringing something with you that they can not offer and do not have. And you will be worth more to us", and added, "you will be the Jackie Robinson for the oil and chemical industry in the Golden Triangle Area. The labor unions also will benefit from your presence".

In all the many companies represented there; Dupont, Goodyear, Gulf Oil, BF Goodrich, Firestone, Mobile, Pure Oil, there was not a single Black working in any technical field in any of these industries. All the Blacks were assigned to labor gangs. Unfortunately, very soon after starting to work for Goodyear, I developed a health problem. I was born with a congenital health problem, of which we had been unaware.

Up until my time with Goodyear, I had been living and working in a fully air-conditioned environment. I had never had the discomfort of perspiring while on the job, which now created a kidney problem. I ran an extremely high body temperature and white blood count, and since this was rare, it took the doctors several weeks to determine what the real problem was. I was transferred back and forth between the Huntsville and Houston hospitals. I was finally stabilized but I was kept in the hospital for more than four weeks. I had agreed to an exploratory operation, which uncovered a birth defect, requiring an extensive operation.[17] In time I returned to work, but I had had time to think while recuperating and decided to organize my home community.

I felt deeply touched by the racism to which I had been exposed and knew that I would never be content with walking away from problems and conditions that had so harshly affected my life. I couldn't just leave this for others, including my children, to do something about it. It was up to me. I decided to dedicate some of my time to making a change. If I didn't do it, who would? If not me, who? When would my world begin to change for the better? What would be the future for my children and their children and your children also? Not only are the Blacks suffering from racism, but many others are suffering too. Many times I had heard a White person speaking to my dad, and end by saying, "Well, Jesse, you know how it is". So often and so many times this statement has been made to me or simply made in my presence. Yes, we "know how it is", but what are we going to do about it"? Racism, under any condition, is not acceptable. Pain is not a pleasure! I asked myself, how can I smile when others are hurting? I had pledged "my life" by going abroad to save a democracy and then was denied democratic process on my return. It became my intention to put meaning into the pledge of allegiance.

While eating syrup and pancakes one Sunday morning with my wife, I was reminded of the ribbon cane syrup we had made on our farm. Each year we raised enough sugar cane to make two to three thousand gallons of syrup. There was an elderly fellow, Lou "Tip" Hightower, who had a singular talent for cooking the syrup. My dad thought his was the best.

Uncle Lou, as we called him, had a special crew of helpers (including me) that consisted of two youngsters and two grown men. One of the men's jobs was to press the juice out of the stalks of cane. We called it "grinding the juice" because we had a cane mill powered by mules that pressed the juice from the cane stalks. The other adult would assist Uncle Lou in the sheds with the skimming of the broth from the evaporating pan. As young boys, our job was to take the juice from the grinder to the sheds and to keep the fire going under their evaporating pan. Keeping the right amount of fire was of utmost importance because too much heat would "scorch" the syrup, ruin the smooth tan color and affect the flavor.

But there was another side to this process, which I'll call "sound" side. It would usually take us from two to three weeks to process all of our cane into syrup, but it was a large cash crop for our family. During the late afternoons 10 to 15 White families would drive out to the mill to watch the operation, drink fresh "cane juice" from the mill, and buy several gallons of syrup to take home. The cane juice was free but the syrup was 50 cents per gallon, which they gladly paid. One of the families had a son, Jack Felder, who was my age and we became the best of friends. His family owned Felder's Dry Goods store in Huntsville where my parents traded. As one of the little "juice boys" around the mill, I was at the "mill" when there was work to be done even if it required my missing school. Jack Felder and his family enjoyed the "mill setting" so much that they would come every evening after they had closed the store. Late each afternoon when no more fire or fresh juice was needed, my dad would let Jack and me go to the "lot" where we kept the calves away from the "milk cows", and ride the calves. Often Jack's parents would bring Jack's little "White friends", and there would be a half a dozen of us 8 to 12 years old riding calves and having fun. For several years of my young life this was a special season for me and I thought I had some real close "White buddies". I continued to believe this into my adult life until I became disillusioned.

I had become involved in the process of getting "my people" to vote and make a difference in their lives. We, "The Walker County Voters League",[18] had on several occasions, approached the Huntsville Independent School District board about the lack of interest in complying with the law of integrating our public schools. A Black Methodist Minister who had moved to Huntsville, Rev. Lee A. Thiegpen, had made some very selfish and unbecoming statements in the community about our Black teachers. He decided to meet with members of the school board personally and help them with their plan for integration. I was in Beaumont when I was informed that he had called a meeting of Blacks so the school representatives could talk to them.[19] I contacted the Health Education and Welfare Department of the U. S. Government and they sent a representative with me to attend that meeting. Guess who represented the school board saying they would not integrate? Jack Felder, Buster Besada and Mance Park. Jack Felder, my supposed "best friend" from childhood, made me ashamed, angry, and bitter.

We had two nine-year old boys, equipped with tape recorders, sitting in the front row directly in line with the speakers. These youngsters managed to get every word that was spoken by, first, Reverend Theigpen, followed by Jack Felder, Buster Besada, and Mance Park. That evening I got one of the greatest lessons of my life, but I will never give up! I have known so many wonderful gracious and caring people who are completely open-minded.

My experience has shown clearly that most people have a desire to be fair and impartial. Neither religion, race, education, social status, skin color, nor language has an affect on their being fair and impartial. I will never let myself believe that most people are bad. The people are the ones who hold our society together, they enrich our lives and add joy and confidence to our future.

I had no training in how to go about it, but I knew it was time for CHANGE! There were some organizations already existing within the community, such as churches and social clubs with pastors, presidents, treasurers and others with influence. I called a meeting of about forty of the people in these capacities, to whom I had spoken and they all agreed to attend. At meeting time only about eight people showed up. I talked with the eight and they listened with intensity to my ideas of how we could work together and what we could accomplish.

I gave each of these eight persons a list of the names of people to whom I had talked and who had promised to come, but didn't. I had those present to understand that "great oaks" begin with "acorns" and they were to be the acorns from which these towering trees would come. The mighty oceans of the earth can be measured in terms of drops of water. The distance across our universe can be measured in inches. I told them we must go back to these people and continue to talk about our future as I had talked to them. Never mention our disappointment in their not being here with us- talk positive, impart information! Keep going in the directions we are trying to go. We're climbing a mountain, not digging a hole. If you talk negatively to people about "their problem" it makes them uncomfortable and they will shut you out and avoid you. You cannot build interest, trust and confidence when this happens. We must become informed so that we can pass the information on to our friends, who in turn will enjoy passing it on to others whom we do not know. When others learn a new source of information they will seek more information from that source. They will begin calling and corning to you when they have a need. When this happens, you become a source of leadership and information. "Let's call this a resource". We must build on this practice and show our people that we can make a difference.

With the many negative racist things that had happened to me in my lifetime, I became very aggressive but above all I tried to maintain an attitude of making changes. Make these changes within the system, only compromise when you are accomplishing something because only results count, excuses do not. After starting to work for Goodyear, I sat down and figured out a system of events that would make differences. I would no longer let things remain the same for my children and others coming after me.

We started with a Poll Tax drive to get people registered to vote. We made assignments to the people present as to what blocks and streets they would work for one needed a Poll Tax receipt to qualify as a voter. The tax was one dollar and seventy-five cents and could only be paid from November 1 through January 31. The Poll Tax was designed to keep the poorer people from voting and as most of the people were farmers or had farm related jobs, they had no income during this period of the year. If the tax was not paid at this time or your receipt was lost you could not vote. We were successful in getting people to register to vote because they had an interest in doing so. We managed to register more than 73% of the Blacks in Walker County, who were old enough to vote. The Blacks were 42% of the population of Walker County. The percentage of Blacks registered made up 65% of the total voters in the County. This enabled us to win every election in which we participated.

We decided to begin working on matters that would improve our community and lift the status of the Blacks. The best way to accomplish this was to work within the system and to deal with the people who made the decisions. We started with the integration of Sam Houston State University by arranging for Annie Kizzie to apply but she was turned down. She was told that the school's bylaws stated that the school was for the education of White youth only.

It wasn't long before we found another student to apply who could be admitted as a transfer student. Her name was Maxine Hayward,[20] who was a teacher in the Willis, Texas Public School system. Her race was not revealed until her transcript arrived from one of the Black colleges. Though she had originally been sent a letter thanking her for her application and interest in coming to Sam Houston State, after receiving her transcript she was sent another letter informing her that she would not be accepted.

She forwarded this letter to me, and upon its receipt, I called a meeting and it was decided to file a lawsuit against the University. When the notice was printed in the paper it accomplished the desired effect and immediately generated considerable interest. As a result, a young man named John Patrick,[21] who was an honor student of his graduating class, was invited to register and he became the first Black student to attend Sam Houston State University.

Chapter Six

SCHOOL DESEGREGATION AND APPLICABLE ATTITUDES

The Supreme Court's ruling in the case of *Brown vs. Board of Education of Topeka* took place on May 17, 1954, but until 1962 the Huntsville community totally ignored the verdict of the Supreme Court. Things began to happen but not for the better. Immediately following that historic decision, our school Superintendent, Dr. Joseph Griggs, was asked when would Huntsville desegregate its schools? He stated, "We won't be the first, but we definitely won't be the last," which aroused Huntsville's racist element, which immediately sought to replace him. The Huntsville Independent School District board found what they wanted in a coach who had steered his high school to a State Championship in football, and then moved on as an Assistant at another school. They hired him to carry their torch.[22]

The State of Texas called a special session of the legislature to deal with school desegregation. Dr. Earl Huffer, a retired college professor, had become our State Representative and Bill Moore of Bryan, Texas was our State senator. These legislators were certainly not an asset for the education of Black Youth and the legislative results of that summer session proved it. The Legislature spent the better part of the summer making deals and passing regressive laws to thwart integration. Among their chicanery, it was decided to let local school districts hold local option elections to decide whether they wanted to comply or not.

Subsequently, they found our voice and our votes expressed our will to survive. With little to say about school desegregation we decided to "go to the top" where the money came from. Each year when the school district applied for Federal funds, we already knew what changes to expect, because we had begun to set the tone and not they. We stayed in close touch with their federal sources of revenue and kept them informed of the progress or the lack of progress in our community. As a result, they got no money until they complied with the law. It was suggested by the U. S. Department of Education that we keep them fully informed of all activities related to the integration process in Huntsville. We would send them a copy of all information gleaned from our local papers. Whenever meetings were held in Huntsville, or when a request was made for money for the operation of our public schools, we would pass that information on so that it was already in the files of the federal officials.

The Superintendent called a meeting at the Chamber of Commerce office to announce his plan for integration. He had selected the Blacks whom he wanted to attend and asked them to be present. As the plan presented to them stated, only one or two Black children could apply, but first the parents "of a seven year-old Black child" would have to request the enrollment through the Black principal and if he approved, he would pass the request on to a White principal and if he approved, it would be passed on to the Superintendent for his approval.

First the parent would be required to tell them where they worked and for whom they worked. The child would be inspected for his/her cleanliness and manners. Only one or two youngsters would be allowed to apply even under these conditions. If the child was able to meet all this criteria, no more than one or two would be accepted. (One must keep in mind that this applies to six and seven year old children who had never been away from their parents before, starting school for the first time in their lives. How cruel can humans behave toward each other?)

I must remind you that this was the plan presented at the Chamber of Commerce office accepted by those attending. These were our leaders!

Wendell Baker

Wendell Baker in 1945, after he joined the military as a Surgical Tech in the U. S. Army Medical Corps. Photo courtesy of the Baker family.

Chapter Seven

CIVIL RIGHTS ACTIVITY BEGINS: JOB AND EDUCATIONAL PROGRESS

These were the type of things that led to our going to the streets with the marches and sit-ins and the affiliation with SCLC and the local group called Ha-You.[23] We became a paid affiliated group under the leadership of Dr. Martin Luther King. We soon had the leadership of Thomas Lichtin, a Harvard student who lived in Dallas, and J. D. Gregory, who was a student of Lamar University. We also had Gilbert Campos, a student from the University Of Houston. We had Rev. James Bevel, Rev. Richard Boone, Rev. William B. Oliver, pastor of a church in Beaumont, Texas. Booker T. Bonner was our final leader and the one who stayed with us through our final chapter of the direct action.

The First Black Employed By the Prison System

Another major problem in the community was the availability of jobs for Black people. Huntsville is the home of the Texas prison system, which at that time didn't have a single Black on its payroll. In a Voters League meeting one night, we brought up the subject of the Texas prison system housing 50% or more Blacks, and yet there were no job opportunities for Black people. Every person employed by the Texas prison system was White. We had Blacks who were attending our meetings who were not in accord with some of our ideas. When we announced that we were going to pursue this issue they quickly arranged to have a meeting the next morning with County Judge Amos Gates, for as they said, "We can't let that Voters League get credit for everything!"[24] Judge Gates invited them to come to his office and they informed him that the Voters League was about to start problems because there were no Blacks working for the prison system. The Judge informed O. B. Ellis, Director of the Prison system.[25] Ellis instructed the judge to send him somebody Black and he would hire him. The Judge sent his maid's son to the prison office and he became the first and only Black hired in less than 24 hours. This young man, Uriah Mayes, was a recent graduate of Sam Houston High School where he had been an excellent student. Later, he told me how badly he had been treated by his superior officers who used racist statements in front of him but never directly resorted to calling him racist names. It was a daily occurrence, even from White prisoners with the officer's approval, but getting him hired was all that we needed. Today, the Texas Department of Criminal Justice not only hires more Blacks than anybody in the State but it is also the largest employer of Blacks.

There was only one retail store in Huntsville, the Grand Leader dry goods store, which had a Black salesperson on the floor, Ruthie Lee Moseley (Nauls). We found that we didn't have to boycott but one grocery store for soon the Blacks were working everywhere.[26] The store we boycotted had a Black man, Sonny Crooks, who swept the floor and dusted cans and shelves. One day outside management came to check the store and found they had employed a Black man. They proceeded to tell the local management that that would not be tolerated. So, Sonny Crooks was fired. We boycotted that store. They closed and moved to a new location. We continued to boycott. Today they are hiring Blacks. Sonny Crooks, who lived and worked in the Mt. Zion community proved to be a dynamic member of our Voters League.[27]

The First Black School Trustee.

The Mt. Zion community was the first to speak out on racial issues in education even before the Walker County Voters League was organized. Many of the schools in Walker County were still operating under the "Common" School District, which was run by a County School Superintendent who was elected by a vote of the people in that County. Each community elected local people called trustees, who chose the teachers and oversaw the maintenance of their local school. Generally these schools were poorly furnished and their programs substandard. The problem was, we still had families in the communities who were big landholders, because they still owned and operated the land that their forefathers had been given when Texas still belonged to Mexico. As a result of this, these families held sway over their communities because they controlled the land, taxes, and jobs.

To teach in Texas, at that time, one only needed to complete a high school education, get a personal recommendation from three people, apply through the county school superintendent for a teacher's certificate, and get hired by the local trustees. As a result of this system, our schools were inferior, for they would start school during the summer and close them in the fall when they wanted their cotton picked. Many of the landowners had their own stores, which enabled them to control the price of the gasoline and groceries sold to their teachers. In some instances, they shared the teacher's monthly salary! This community got tired of getting "the neck of the chicken" and elected Toy Archie, the first Black, to their board of trustees. The local election was being held in the home of one of the original trustees and they either did not permit the Blacks to come, or the Blacks chose not to go to that home due to the racial climate. The Blacks held their own election, in compliance with state standards, voted in greater numbers and their candidate was declared the winner by the state education agency.

Cheating the Huntsville Independent School District Cafeteria workers out of their pay.

It was called to my attention by a White cafeteria worker in a Huntsville public school that they wanted to promote her to a new position where she would be over several of the Black workers. She had been told that at their break time she was to have the Blacks stay in the kitchen to watch over the cooking. She, in turn, told the school administration that she considered that to be stealing those people's labor and she wouldn't do it. They fired her. She informed me and I filed with the U. S. Labor Department in Beaumont which transferred my complaint to the Dallas office. Eventually some inspectors showed up, got the records, talk to these cafeteria workers, and subpoenaed their records. Upon learning it was true they sent the Huntsville Independent School District a directive informing them of the amount of back time they owed each worker. The superintendent told the workers that the people doing the investigations were from their insurance company. He later came back with money and told them that this was money being sent to them by their insurance company for not having had any claims for accidents. They accepted what he gave them and signed a release. So this closed their case, though they had been lied to and cheated.

Baker at his 1949 graduation from Texas State College for Negroes, now Texas Southern University. Photo courtesy of the Baker family.

Chapter Eight

MAKING A DIFFERENCE
BY POLITICAL INVOLVEMENT
(Hospital Election, Election Official, Housing Project)

The First Black Elected to the Hospital District Board of Managers.

Wendell Baker was elected to the Walker County Hospital District Board of Managers for five 2-year terms.[28] During which time things happened to cause other managers of the board to vote with him. There was a problem of properly serving our community during the birth of babies, for we had unwed mothers with no insurance and no medical attention until delivery. Usually the doctors had no prior knowledge of most of these patients and many of them had not seen a doctor because the cost was prohibitive. Since many of these expectant mothers could not pay for the care they needed they waited and showed up at the hospital as an emergency case at the time of delivery. This posed a serious medical problem and unnecessary risks for the patients and doctors. A clinic was established in Huntsville under the supervision of the University of Texas Medical Branch of Galveston. Today expectant mothers are getting the care they need even when unable to pay. Progress of this sort was accomplished because the voters supported me. I prefer to use the terms "we" and "us" and not just "me", for though I might have come up with the ideas, many people, Black and White, made it work. I had wonderful cooperation and support from the other members on the hospital board.

Working the Polls on Elections: What an experience!

When Lyndon Johnson ran against Barry Goldwater for the Presidency, it brought about a new day in Walker County.[29] We knew this would be a hotly challenged election in Huntsville because of its racial overtones. No Black had worked the polls since Reconstruction days. In fact, most Blacks had not ever voted.

Father Al Johnson, a well-educated dynamic friend and pastor of the local Episcopal Church, taught me the "ins and outs" of the electoral process.[30] I shared his expertise with others and took my neighbors to the polls, but I had not as yet become interested in learning the laws or election code of Texas. A group of young white students on the campus organized as the Young Democrats were working with Father Al. With their help it was decided that I should make an attempt to work at the polls, as Blacks had never been included. I was to become a "poll watcher". Now, there were three methods by which an individual could become a poll watcher.

One – He could get a candidate to request it but the poll watcher could only work at the poll where he was qualified to vote. Two – He could get documents signed by three members of the County Democratic Committee which would qualify him to work as poll watcher in his voting precinct. Three – If his documents were signed by the County Democratic Chairman that person could work at any polling place in the county.

Several students acquired the blank forms and got one of the candidates to sign them. Because they were White students, the candidate assumed the poll watcher would be a White person. The papers were blank except for the candidate's signature and name. The students then took another blank application to three members of the County Democratic Committee who also unknowingly signed the blank application. Keep in mind that with these credentials, one could only work the voter precinct where one was qualified to vote.

Just before the midnight deadline, these students went to the Democratic Chairman for his signature, which he graciously signed, no questions asked. In fact, he made the students feel there would be no problem. My name was on this document.

As soon as the students got his signature and left the County Chairman called my home and told me he didn't want me at the polls. The students had written the designation of the polling place on this form, so he knew who I was and knew the place where I would be working had almost no Black voters. I was noncommittal, so the chairman called me a second time and told me what a good man the election judge was and that he wouldn't need my help or to be watched. I still made no promises. At 5:00 a.m. he called for the third time and told me I could NOT work at that polling place and NOT to show up! I, in turn, informed him that the election code states, "If the County Chairman signs the application, this qualifies one to work at any polling place under his jurisdiction." I again made no promises. He hung up. The polls were to open by 7:00 a.m. I left home before 5:30 a.m., as we needed to be at the polling place by 6:00 to set up the tales. The Chairman called again but my wife told him she was unsure of where I was but when the polls opened, I would be there! He cursed! Actually I had gone to Father Al's house for coffee and donuts with him and two carloads of students.

I drove to the polling place followed by 10 young white men in two other cars. They told me, "Mr. Baker, we don't want you to be hurt. We will be with you the rest of the day so if any problem arises inside the polling place, just come to the door and give us a signal and let us do the rest". When I got off at 7:15 p.m. one of the young men started my car for me and followed me home. Earlier that morning when the door was unlocked to open up the polls, we had all walked into the building together. The voting was held in the gym of the White High School. Father Al, who was also a lawyer, followed us to the polling place but did not stand near us.

After setting up the room, the election judge called for everyone to come up and bring their credentials so he could swear us in but when he got to me he yelled at me, "Get out"! Father Al spoke up saying, "Sir, I am an Attorney at Law, and this is my client. On what grounds are you refusing his credentials?" With this the Election Judge started to mumble but Father Al just stepped closer and pointed a finger in his face saying, "I demand an answer! On what grounds sir?" The Election Judge told him the County Chairman had told him to refuse me. Father Al said, "I will go have counsel with your County Chairman and this man had better be here when 1 get back." With that he stormed out of the building. I quietly took a seat and started reading a magazine that I had brought with me. After about 30 minutes the chairman called to me and said, "Wendell, I will accept your credentials." I handed them to him, he swore me in and I went to work.

Under the election code rules, I could only talk to the election judge if I saw something going wrong. I soon observed several things going wrong! I had a copy of the election code in my pocket, and though I remained polite and well mannered, each time I called his attention to a violation he would watch me write it down and check the time. The judge soon knew that I was well versed in the rules and he came to me whenever the other workers had a question. Very soon we had a harmonious day.

We helped Black people who were blind, or who could not read the ballots. Family members were allowed to assist their relatives, by taking ballots out to the cars to those who were too ill to come in. Most of the people who we were helping were Black, but when I saw that Whites who didn't live in that precinct were being allowed to vote, we increased our efforts to bring in more Blacks.

During the morning several Whites were getting themselves ready to remove me forcibly from the polls. Unfortunately they went to the *Huntsville Item* and told Ross Woodall, the editor, what they planned to do. Edward Owens, a Black man who worked for the *Item*, was working out of sight under a counter when he overheard their conversation. One of the men said, "Ross, there is a nigger up at the gym disrupting the election. We're going up there and put him out. We thought you might go with us". Ross replied, "Fellows, you know I don't like that any more than you do, but I'm not going up there and I would advise you not to go up their either. That boy is protected by the Federal Government and has every right to be there. If you bother that man you will never get out of trouble the longest day you live. I'm not going and I would advise that you don't go." They stood silently for a moment and then told Ross Woodall they would see him and left.

Since then our Voters League has elected 15 of the 16 election judges and others to the County Democratic Committee. Many have been Blacks including Maultie Rolling, J. C. Phillips, Mrs. Hattye Owens, Mrs. Lucy Mason Willis, myself and now Floyd Ross of Precinct 2. All of us were elected to consecutive terms.

Federal Housing Project on Martin Luther King Drive and how it started

After the Voters League had proven that we could produce winners in an election, we had many good people who came to us and asked for our support. Several of us in the Voters League had checked on housing projects in Diboll and Cleveland, Texas. When we returned to Huntsville we contacted a councilman and asked why Huntsville didn't use federal money for low cost housing. Of course he hadn't thought about it, but his answer was, "Let me handle it". By this, I knew that he was suggesting that I should not go before the City Council in person because most elected officials would feel that {I} we were putting pressure on them which would make them uncomfortable and they wouldn't want it to appear that we could force them to make decisions. Within a few days this councilman came back to me and said they had found some land, which they were trying to buy and the housing project would be built. This councilman said he had mentioned this idea to a couple of the Council Members who in turn had some ideas of things that they wanted to achieve. By building a coalition of friends and ideas on the council with him, he was able to make this an easy project to pass. There are many, many wonderful people who want to do the right thing who are looking for good things to do for others. They find it is rewarding to share their dreams with others for the benefit of all.

Chapter Nine

PAVING STREETS AND VOTING THE CITY "WET"

Paving the Streets All Over Town
One time, after a fast and hard summer evening thunderstorm, I called a City Councilman who had asked and received our support to go with me to see something. I took him to a street that was flowing like a creek and explained that the residents had to use it daily to go to work. They deserved something better. He said he would see what he could do and get back to me. I thought he had forgotten, but in a couple of weeks I went to the site and there were several pieces of road building equipment. The project had begun. He told me that the council had passed a resolution that all streets in the city would be paved and whenever annexation took place the first order of business would be to pave the street. This meant that all those little narrow streets in the Black neighborhoods would now be improved and they were.

Life's piano can only produce the harmony of brotherhood when we recognize that the black keys are as basic, necessary, and beautiful as the white keys as we accept and appreciate each other. We invite the opportunity to participate in the beauty of diversity.

Voting the City Wet, and a church city at that
At one time a favorite form of gossip around town was who was arrested or who got beaten up going and coming to Trinity to buy alcohol. In order to get a wet-dry election it took a percentage of the number of voters in the affected area that had voted in the governor's race in the last election to sign a petition. Now this being a "church city", nobody wanted his or her name on a petition requesting a liquor election. We had already made it legal for 18 year olds to vote for I strongly believed if 18 year olds could serve in the military and face death around the world, 18 year olds should be permitted to make a choice on who sends him there.

We hosted a party that attracted a large group of young college students and urged them to register to vote. Many of them filled out voter registration forms which we duly submitted and their authentic voter certificate was issued. We then contacted them and urged them to sign the petition to have a liquor election.[31] When the County Commissioners decided they would not act on that petition we informed them that they had no choice. Action was required by law. Signing up the students gave us the required number of signatures from qualified voters who were not embarrassed to request a liquor election and didn't mind their names being published. There had been a threat made in the community that the list of names signing the petition would be published in the local newspaper. Those college students involved didn't mind that. The election passed and stores that previously had not sold liquor are doing so today.

Refusal to sell this beautiful home that Baker built on his own land resulted in Baker's dismissal from his Huntsville teaching position at the end of the 1960-1961 school year. Photo courtesy of the Baker family.

Chapter Ten

CHANGING AVENUE F TO MARTIN LUTHER KING

One day I walked into the house of George Perry (GP), a former student of mine who was currently a very conscientious worker in the Voters League. He asked me, "Mr. Baker, why can't we get that street named Martin Luther King"? I phoned the City Manager, and was told that there had been opposition to the name change so they had tabled it. With that, I asked for it to be put on the agenda for the next meeting so I could address the Council.

When I arrived at the meeting I noticed that my name was not on the agenda, but that a Black City Council person was slated to address the name change. In his presentation he asked that the street name remain the same except for a stretch down in the woods where there were no buildings. Nothing! He recommended that the street remain Avenue F for the sake of "peace and harmony, which as you know, Dr. King stood for". When he had finished the council voted 100% for his presentation. I became very upset because he had this project for about 2 years and had done absolutely nothing about it until I asked to be on the agenda. Immediately after his presentation and vote a recess was called and the council members came over to shake my hand. I refused. I told them I was "most unhappy" and we wouldn't accept it. I also told them that I was going from there to the Greater Zion Baptist Church where the men were holding a meeting and, that we would have a recall election in Huntsville if needed. A recall election would have meant that we would get up a petition which would require the Council to again run for office against whoever we put up as candidates even though the Councils terms had not expired. Then I walked out of the meeting.

Before daylight the following morning the mayor, Jane Monday[32] called my friend Cecil Williams,[33] who was our Black County Commissioner, and asked him to see what it would take to straighten out this matter. We were to arrange a meeting with the councilman and she would see that he attended. We set a time and place for the meeting but the councilman "didn't show". When Cecil reported this to the mayor she became very upset.

Cecil was then instructed to set another time and place for this meeting to inform her when and she would personally see to it that he attended. For the next appointment Cecil Williams, Richard Watkins and I walked into the appointed place and the Councilman was sitting waiting for us. We walked directly up to him and I announced, "Avenue F will be named Martin Luther King with no ifs, ands, or buts, and I don't think you want to object to that!" I was notified of the next City Council meeting and this time the Councilman presented it "My Way". It passed with 100% of the council votes. Today the street is Martin Luther King, and there is a named building, "The Martin Luther King Recreation Center."

Wendell Baker was a broadcaster for KSAM, a Huntsville, Texas radio station, from 1953 to 1961. He lost his job at the station shortly after his dismissal from teaching. Photo courtesy of the Baker family.

Chapter Eleven

ELECTING COUNTY COMMISSIONER

Our First Black County Commissioner Since Reconstruction.

Cecil Williams was a native of Huntsville and the son of Maggie Williams, a teacher, and Lester Williams, a farmer, so it's OK to call him a "country boy". He got his public school education in Walker County and went on to Prairie View A&M College. After a stint in the Army he returned, finished his college work and started teaching in the county schools, ending up in time in the Huntsville Independent School District. Because he was a farmer himself, he was a very effective and interesting agricultural teacher. Through his farm club, the New Farmer of America, his students developed skills in mechanics, bookkeeping, chapter conducting, singing, public speaking and carpentry.

His "Ag Boys," as they were called, won many awards and honors, for one of Cecil's talents was his ability to get other teachers to work with him.

Cecil's Ag Club quartets won championships year after year starting with district, then bi-district, state, area, and on to National Championship. Once they became State Champions, they couldn't compete anymore, so he saved that for the boys in his senior classes. These boys were also winners in football, basketball, track, and other sports. Once the boys got the spirit and joy of being the best, that's what they wanted to be.

In time Cecil became an Assistant Principal and later the Principal of Adult Education. Actually, someone had been brought in for the position of Principal and was being introduced to the community. We sent a letter to the board members reviewing Cecil's success and ability in this field and we believe this made the difference. Cecil headed the Adult Education Department until his retirement.

The Republicans in Walker County were trying to become recognized as a viable organization. We had heard that the State Republican machine would not spend any money on a candidate in Walker County because they felt they couldn't win. Cecil was urged to run for a position in the Republican Party but he was reluctant. We talked to him about the history of Black Republicans in Texas and Walker County and about our strategy to make him a winner. The Democrat (White) serving in this commissioner's post had received considerable negative publicity so we encouraged Cecil to run in the Republican Primary while we supported the failing incumbent in the Democratic Primary. The Republicans had another candidate who filed but the party machine asked him to step down and not to run against Cecil, which he did. We knew that it would be very difficult to get most Blacks to vote Republican on anything, so we urged them to support the failing incumbent in the Democratic Primary. As hoped, Cecil won the Republican Ticket, and the failing incumbent won the Democratic Ticket.

Now, we knew that we could get the angry White Democrats and the Republicans together for Cecil, plus be able to get many of our Blacks to split the ticket. This accomplished, Cecil was elected as our first Black County Commissioner since the early 1900's. This also gave Walker County its first Republican County Judge. Through the years, as a voter group, we interceded for several other worthy Blacks for various positions.

Chapter Twelve

COUNTY AGENT PROMOTION

Stop Passing Over Our County Agent, and why?

Our Black County Agent, Hugh Epps, proved to be an excellent well qualified agent. When the White agent who had held the position was promoted, Mr. Epps was moved into his position, but when another White person was found to take the position, Mr. Epps was demoted. This happened twice! Mr. Epps was handling the agent's job competently when another attempt was made to demote him. We informed the Commissioner's Court we were watching and expected Epps to retain the job. I wrote to each County Commissioner, all of whom I knew to be fine people, but they probably would not have made the decision they did had we not interceded. We also sent copies to Mr. Epps immediate district superior, higher up "on the totem pole" in College Station and the "Powers That Be" in Austin, Texas. Mr. Epps received the position that he deserved. He stood with great dignity, and professionalism, and proved to be great inspiration to all of us. He retired at the top of his profession.

The poll tax was a significant barrier to political participation for many minority and poor citizens. Baker and others organized "The Walker County Voters' League" to overcome the barriers to participation. This 1927 receipt is the type that needed not only to be purchased, but also brought to the polling place. Photo courtesy of the Baker family.

Chapter Thirteen

PRINCIPAL'S PROMOTION

Earnest Grover as Principle of the Elementary School-No leadership qualities-- by whose measurements?

The White Principal, who was the principal of the junior high school that was formerly an all-black high school, died. We had a competent Black Assistant Principal in Earnest Grover. When the School Board brought in an outsider for the job and introduced him to the community, I contacted the Chairperson of the board and asked her what was happening. She said she felt Grover was an excellent young man, but that he lacked leadership qualities. I then asked how long had she known this and what had the board tried to do for him? The answer was that the board had recognized it but they hadn't done anything. I then said that I personally felt that Earnest Grover would and could serve in that position as well as anyone. If short comings were noticed, there had been ample opportunity to correct them. Why had they waited until now to make it an issue? I also asked, "Are you saying you find your attitude acceptable and that we can expect this to carry over into all of the principal jobs that come up? If so, you can explain this to the Black community in your next bond issue and board election." Mr. Grover was given the job and served as Principal until his retirement.

Chapter Fourteen

CERTIFYING OUR POLICEMEN and
NO MORE DIME--STORE RECEIPT BOOKS

My youngest sister Leola was a beautician and at one time traveled from Houston to Huntsville to tend to her local customers. Her family owned property in town where the beauty shop was so when she came to Huntsville her three young boys and my children looked forward to meeting at the shop and then going out to the farm.

Being farm-reared, we had all taught our children to drive when they were 12-14 years old. One Saturday when Leola's young son, Sonny, was driving with about six other children in the car, they were stopped by a city policeman who wrote him a ticket. He was told to go back and tell his mother that she had better get down to the county jail and pay it or he would find Sonny and lock him up. Sonny turned the car around and went back and told his mother what the policeman had said. She went to the jail to pay the fine, but when she got there Sheriff Darrell White recognized her and wanted to know why she was there. He then told the dispatcher to call the policeman and have him come and collect this fine. The policeman came and after she paid him he pulled a dime store receipt book from his pocket and wrote her a "receipt" for the fine. When I saw her "receipt" I called the mayor and two other City Council members. On Monday morning, a special session was called for the Council and the City Officials. They returned my sister's money and adopted a resolution saying that the Huntsville Police Department would no longer hire officers who were not trained and certified. Fortunately this broke up a pattern of behavior where city police sat and watched stop signs at night or on weekends. They would write a ticket, set the fine, collect the fine, (which the policemen called a "cash bond"), give a dime store receipt and keep the money. Incidentally, the morning of the council meeting that policeman had not turned in the money for the fine.

This activity was common and most of the people paying fines in this manner were Black. Some had to go through Huntsville from Trinity or other East Texas towns on their way to Houston to their jobs. This shakedown had been going on for some time but no one had questioned it. Keep in mind that the money was called a "cash bond" so if victims didn't come for a court hearing, their money was forfeited. Since the people who were stopped were primarily "working people," they were unable to leave their jobs in Houston to come back here to Huntsville for a traffic fine, which they would surely have had to pay anyway. So they paid the money and went on.

Chapter Fifteen

HUNTSVILLE INDEPENDENT SCHOOL DISTRICT: 4A OR 5A

Huntsville I.S.D. wants to be classified as a 4A school. I guess the number of "eligible students" determines the classification of a public school. However, the system of determining eligibility has many regulations and many violations as well.

The UIL determines and enforces the classification system based on information furnished by the school system. Schools are allowed to discount students for certain activities based on whether they are wheel-chair bound or other similar reasons disqualifying the student from athletic eligibility.

The Huntsville Independent School District was discounting Black students based on their experience in the Challenge Program, an alternative program for students with behavioral problems. I had students tell me that they had been sent to the Challenge Program because a teacher told them to "sit down" and they didn't do it quick enough. The School Board adopted a policy that said, "If a student is sent to the Challenge Program for any reason, that student was no longer qualified to participate in extra-curricular activities. To clarify their intent, it stated, "for example, if a student is sent to the Challenge Program in the 9th grade, he or she cannot participate in the 10th, 11th, or 12th grades." This disqualified the student for the rest of his/her high school career.

The purpose for this regulation was not only to keep Huntsville Independent School District classified as a 4A school but was also in place because, as a member of the community stated, "As long as the niggers are playing, the white boys could not get to play and develop and get these good scholarships to their Colleges and Universities, so we have to give our boys a chance to play." As this conversation continued, it was said that, "the coaches would have to win some games, or they won't have a job." So they decided that Huntsville Independent School District would go to Class 4A by reducing the school district's student count.

When I was informed of this I confronted the school superintendent and he said the U.I.L. "made them do it." Then I had a personal friend of mine, who was high up in state government call the U.I.L. on my behalf. Within two hours I had in my hand a copy of a letter from U.I.L. to the head of the Athletic Department of Huntsville I.S.D. that said, "The head of the Athletic Department, the Superintendent, several of your principals, and board members asked us to let you do that, and we permitted you to do so."

This letter said "At the end of this term, you will no longer be permitted to do that." The next day the head of the Athletic Department resigned.

I now know that all students can participate in Huntsville Independent School District's extracurricular activities.

This portrait is Wendell Baker during his years as a chemist at Goodyear and courageous activist in Walker County. Photo courtesy of the Baker family.

Chapter Sixteen

MY ONE CONVICTION

When one "rocks the boat" one becomes a sitting duck and an attempt to take that person out can occur at any time.

It was early summer and a run-off election was being held. On the first day of voting I was in the office of a local real estate dealer very early in the morning and he decided that I needed to get some papers from the County Clerk's office. I was at the Clerk's door before it opened as were about fifteen other people who were waiting to vote before going to work.

When the door opened we all rushed in and those wishing to vote asked for ballots. I asked for the papers I needed. However, since it would take a while for the Clerk's Office to find what I needed the clerk asked if I would stand back and let him get the ballots for the voters. I agreed! While waiting I got my voter registration card from my pocket and proceeded to vote. After that I got the papers I needed and left.

I also went back to my job in Beaumont, Texas and worked seven nights consecutively from 11:00pm to 7:00am.

Our public schools were integrated and quite a few of our Black students were doing fine in school, making excellent grades and participating in extracurricular activities. It was decided by a group of us that we would have a picnic for them. I had access to buying much of what we needed at wholesale prices. So I stayed up all day that Thursday and worked all night that Thursday night, then drove my car from Beaumont to Huntsville. I was suffering from lack of sleep.

As I get into Cleveland, Texas I picked up the KSAM radio station and turned it up to keep myself awake until I could get to Huntsville.

My daughter, Pamela, was graduating from Nursing School in Atlanta, Georgia and we were to be there for graduation ceremonies scheduled for Saturday morning. When I drove up in my yard everything was packed and ready to load into the car for the trip to Atlanta. I told my daughter, Cima, to drive me to town to vote because this was the last day of voting. I voted, came home, and ate breakfast. The family loaded the car and I got in the back seat and went to sleep. I awakened in southern Alabama because we were out of gas.

We stayed in Georgia for several days and when I returned the district attorney, Frank Blasek, was waiting for me. He had the two sheets where I had signed in to vote copied and waiting for me. My signature was at the top of one page (the first time) and down near the middle of the page (the second time). He asked if each was my signature. My answer was "yes".

I asked what the fine was and offered to pay it. He said to me I could not simply pay a fine and that I would have to have a court trial.

We spent one day selecting the jury and several more days in a "mock trial" that ended up costing Walker County plenty all because I had truly forgotten that I had already voted that morning when I was at the County Clerk's office for another reason. After a week was consumed with my trial I was sentenced to one month in jail and a fine of $200.00.

I did not spend a single day in jail. I spent about two days in the Huntsville hospital and the rest of the time in a hospital in Houston, then released on "good time served." My friends paid the $200.00 and I took the blow for being an agitator and trouble maker.

Finally, in the next election the district attorney lost his job. He also did not get reelected. The County court-at-law judge resigned and DID NOT get the job he resigned for. Votes CAN make a difference!!

Baker standing with Dan Ellis, the Democratic Texas State House of Representatives legislator from District 18; and Richard Watkins, African American leader and local president of the National Association for the Advancement of Colored people in the late 1990s. Photo courtesy of the Baker family.

Chapter Seventeen

FIRING OUR BLACK POLICE WOMAN, DENEEN FORD--FOR WHAT?

Huntsville had a Black woman police officer, Deneen Ford, a caring, talented person. She not only spoke several languages but had a special talent for working with our young boys and keeping them off the streets. Some of her White co-workers began calling her a demeaning name, which she refused to tolerate. Finally it led to a confrontation at which time the police chief fired her. She acquired a lawyer and filed a federal suit for her pride had been hurt. Not satisfied, she decided she wanted her job back too, so she went to the president of the local NAACP who referred her to me. I consented to accompany her at her appeal procedure. The hearing lasted all day but the result was that she recovered her job with no loss of pay or vacation time and had her sick leave restored. But, most importantly what it really did was it automatically won her Federal suit. Actually, there was no trial in the Federal Court for the judge asked her, her attorney, and the city's insurance attorney to arrive at a settlement and report their conclusion. Miss Ford was awarded a handsome sum of money which was paid by the city's insurance company and then awarded another sum of money to resign (which she accepted). This settlement resulted in the media filing a suit to find out what compensation she had received. Deneen was victorious.

Chapter Eighteen

INTEGRATING THE HUNTSVILLE MEMORIAL HOSPITAL: JUST WELL PLANNED, THAT'S ALL

One evening I received a call from some college students who worked at the Huntsville Memorial Hospital. They were concerned for Jerry Jones, President of the local Chapter of the NAACP, who had attempted to enter the hospital on an integrated basis but had been refused. A local doctor told him that he could not have him admitted for "political reasons".

My wife, Augusta, had a minor medical problem that she had discussed with her doctor. I asked her to return to him for another consultation and if he suggested the minor operation as before, they should make an appointment for her to be admitted to the hospital.

The plan worked. I told her that they should decide on a date for the operation and she could call me in Beaumont where I was employed by the Goodyear Chemical Plant. When she called I told my supervisor that I needed to return to Huntsville because my wife was about to have surgery. On arrival, I called her doctor and told him I was here for the procedure that he had advised, but I further stated that I would not accept the "Crow" conditions at the hospital. The hospital had a surgical and a medical ward for the White patients, and a "catch-all" for Blacks. I insisted that my wife be in the surgical ward where she belonged. The doctor said he would have to make a call and get back to me. Later he did call back and say that it almost took an act of congress, but to have her at the hospital at 10:00 p.m. and they would have a room for her.

What had happened was that after Jerry Jones made his move to be admitted by the hospital staff, the doctors and the hospital board had a meeting in which the Board Chairman told the hospital staff to have the doctors assign the beds to take the responsibility off of the hospital staff. Thus it became "doctors orders".

We were admitted at that late hour to a room that had been prepared for her. A man had been moved out of this room and down the hall. When the nurses ushered us into this room the man was standing in the hall watching. After the nurses left the man came back to Augusta's room. I was still there and when he saw me he jumped back out of the doorway. The nurses saw him and told him to return to his room and stay there and if they saw him at our room again they would have him arrested.

A few days later, one of my sons became ill. The doctor sent him to the medical ward where he was put in the same room with an elderly White gentleman. This man and his family were extremely cordial to us. They proved to be wonderful people. This integrated the medical and the surgical wards at Huntsville Memorial Hospital. When Walker County decided to build a new and larger hospital, it appeared that there were no plans to try to have a segregated system again and that problem was erased from our community.

How We Voted In the Hospital District.

Dr. Dorothy Huskey invited me to a meeting at Sam Houston State University concerning the establishment of a hospital district in Walker County.[34] The hospital board had hired attorneys in Houston to draft a bill for the Texas Legislature to establish a Hospital District for Walker County. This bill, known as the "Enabling Act", had been passed by the legislature and had been voted on once and defeated by the voters of Walker County. It was rescheduled for voting again but was sure to fail a second time because it was only about six days away. I told the Chairman of the Hospital Board, Wilburn Robinson, that it would surely again fail this second time because the election was only one week away but if it was brought up again at the end of six months we could pass it.

There was a group of citizens who were against the hospital board because they wanted to build a private hospital in Huntsville. This would have removed the revenue of the insured and paying customers who could support a hospital that would serve everyone. The bill was reintroduced a third time six months later and the Walker County Voters League saw to it that it passed with flying colors. The group, trying to establish the private hospital was roundly defeated. They had equipment doing the foundation work for its hospital, but after the defeat it sat idle for months. No building was done.

Chapter Nineteen

FIRST BLACK CITY COUNCIL PERSON

With the backing and support of the Walker County Voters League, Scott E. Johnson, a former Principal of the Samuel Walker Houston High School, was elected to the Huntsville City Council and served 8 years.

Chapter Twenty

BLACK ELECTED CONSTABLE OF PRECINCT 2

Curtis "Jab" Dickie who had been involved in law enforcement in Harris and Madison Counties was elected Constable of precinct 2 in Walker County.

This family portrait includes the Wendell Baker immediate family. Standing from left to right are Wendell, Jr., Cima, Bruce, and Donald. Seated left to right are Wendell, Sr., Augusta, and Pamela. This was a relaxed and happy occasion. Photo courtesy of the Baker family.

Chapter Twenty-one

ELECTED LOCAL DOCTOR TO CITY COUNCIL

Dr. Frank Vickers, a brilliant young physician who practiced in Huntsville for many years, asked for the Voters League's support for a position on the Huntsville City Council, for he wanted to introduce fluoride into the water supply to help prevent tooth decay. We supported him and he won and served for many years. Huntsville is still adding fluoride to the City Water System.

Chapter Twenty-two

BLACKS ON COUNTY DEMOCRATIC COMMITTEE

With our superior voting strength and having 65% of the registered voters, we were able to start electing precinct chairpersons. Of the 16 available positions in the county we were able to elect 15 people of our choice. This move gave us election judges, and other workers, which greatly enhanced the confidence of Blacks and their involvement in the electoral process. Today, several of the voter boxes are staffed completely by Blacks.

Chapter Twenty-three

OPENING A PRENATAL CLINIC

Before we voted in the hospital district as a taxing entity, the hospital had been run by the county officials, who generally had no knowledge of hospital operations and very little concern about the patient's welfare.

Many of the poorer residents of the county who needed medical care were really political dependents of the system. Poor people receiving medical care were often made to feel that someone was doing them a personal favor. This attitude subjected the people to a feeling of dependency or favoritism.

There were many women who were coming to the hospital for deliveries who had never seen a doctor. This type of operation put the patients at risk and undue responsibility on the medical staff. Through the change to a hospital district we developed a system whereby patients could get the same medical care from the Texas Medical Branch here in our clinic and avoid the long trip to Galveston.

This photo shows a time when political leader James Baker and his spouse, Susan, visited Wendell and Augusta at their home, though Augusta is not in this photo. Earlier, as James reported in his autobiography, *Work Hard, Study . . . and Keep Out of Politics*, he discovered that he was related to Wendell. He also noted that even though their politics did not always agree, they got along well. Photo courtesy of the Baker family.

Chapter Twenty-four

THE SWIMMING POOL EVENT

When cities around the country began to feel the pressure of permitting Blacks to use the parks, swimming pools, golf courses, and other recreational facilities Huntsville gave the operation of the city's swimming pool to the college which was not as yet integrated. When it did become integrated Sam Houston State University gave it back to the city. The City of Huntsville chose to keep it closed until they could come up with something to satisfy the Blacks. To do this, they decided to build a swimming pool for the Blacks at the Emancipation Park. This required the City to hold a bond election to finance it.

In the Voters League meeting I suggested that we support this bond election, which we did and it passed. When the results were announced the Voters League released a statement to the effect that now we had two swimming pools. At that, Huntsville decided not to open the other swimming pool and proceeded to put a fire station over the pool's location.

The City then decided not to build the 2nd pool even though we had passed the bond for the money to do so. This project languished for many years until it was finally decided to build a pool North on Highway 75 near the airport. The bond issue had to be re-voted to use the money at the new site. Today there is an integrated swimming facility on Highway 75 North.

Chapter Twenty-five

"JUNETEENTH" AS A HOLIDAY

The Black Legislative Caucus introduced a bill to get June nineteenth recognized as a legal holiday in Texas.[35] Senator Bill Moore wanted their support for an issue in which he had an interest. Senator Moore requested the support of the Black Legislative Caucus and, in turn, the Black legislators asked for his support. This worked and June 19 became a legal holiday in Texas. Unfortunately we had a foreman in Huntsville's city management who told his Black workers, "If you don't show up for work tomorrow, when you return someone else will have your job!"

Several of these men came to my house that afternoon when they got off from work and told me what the foreman had said, whereupon I immediately called the mayor and two city councilmen who had asked for our support and I asked who made that decision. They were surprised and told me they would call me back. Shortly after, I received a call back from the mayor telling me to let all the Black workers know that their being off would NOT affect their jobs. They could take June 19th off and make it up on any of the other recognized holidays. This eliminated that problem!

Organizing the Walker County Voters League and finding so many honest dedicated workers who believed in and supported the causes we championed was most inspiring for me. I also discovered many people throughout the state of Texas whose leadership I respected and whose ideas I shared.

I want to share the joy of just driving into East Texas towns, not knowing a single person, just stopping in a barber or beauty shop to meet new people, making conversation and after a few passing minutes knowing the names, addresses, phone numbers of the people that they know and respect.

Upon returning home with this information, writing each one a letter inviting them to a meeting in their own town, then going back and seeing new faces who shared my vision and aspirations. What a joy!

Chapter Twenty-six

ORGANIZATION OF VOTER GROUPS

Organizing the Walker County Voters League and our being a part of the East Texas Citizens League and the Texas Council of Voters. I discovered our community was ahead of the curve with many of the plans we proposed or had executed. At a peak in our activity as the Walker County Voters League and the East Texas Citizens League (which I had also organized) we embarked on a new adventure. The Blacks in Houston who were involved in The Harris County Council Of Organizations were faced with a dilemma. Texas U. S. Senator Price Daniels wanted to become the Governor of Texas, but due to the six-year terms of Senators and the shorter term of Governors, Price Daniels had to run on the Democratic ticket for both positions. He entered his name in the primary and won both positions so at the beginning of his term as Governor he had to resign his position as Senator. It was then required of the Texas Democratic Party to appoint a successor to the Senate until the next general election at which time the appointee would have to run for the Senate seat.

When the time came to make that appointment, the Texas Democratic Machine refused to let the Texas Council of Voters, AFL-CIO or the Mexican American voters group participate in that meeting. A very conservative man from the Dallas area was appointed.[36] He served the one-year but then was required, by law, to run for the office. This drew a Republican opponent who was John Tower.[37]

The Harris County Council of Organizations considered forming a second group, to be known as the "Texas Black Republicans" and for this they were banned from the meeting. Their feeling was that the Democrat who had been appointed to serve that year had not represented their interest and was a racist who the Council did not want to support. I was called and asked if I would help get a group of Blacks to attend a meeting in Houston. The Republican Party would pay for their travel and food expenses.

I had a huge mailing list of Blacks throughout the 31 counties I had organized into the East Texas Citizens League. I sent letters to about 200 members and the morning of the meeting at the Astroworld Hotel we found that we could not get all those people into the room. A suite of 2 rooms down the hall was located but within an hour it could not hold the crowd. We then found it necessary to get the ballroom at the Astroworld Hotel. With help of 5 secretaries we were able to get all those people registered about 10:00 a.m.

I had instructed the people I had invited to bring the letter that they received from me so they could be reimbursed for their travel. When we broke for lunch we had them turn in their letters to determine their travel costs and receive their lunch tickets. Then, when they were ready to leave they could pick up the money for their travel. This worked - John Tower won the election and served for many years. Many Blacks were appointed to the FHA, SBA and Postal Service; appointments that Blacks had never held before.

This photo was taken in 2003, when Wendell Baker was eighty one years old. That was his age when he wrote his thoughtful book, *If Not Me, Who?* Photo courtesy of the Baker family.

CHAPTER Twenty-Seven

A HIGHLIGHT IN MY LIFE: THE MILLION MAN MARCH

Before ending this saga, I wish to state that one of the most inspiring experiences of my life was to attend the Million Man March in Washington, D. C.[38] It was an exhilarating experience to have been a part of this tremendous group. When the idea of the Million Man March was first announced I causally mentioned to my wife that I would like to attend such an event. The publicity that this proposed activity was getting nation wide and the negative attitude taken by many Church leaders, particularly in the Houston area, motivated me even more.

My wife mentioned my interest in the presence of my oldest son, Wendell Jr. He told her that he would provide this experience at no expense to me and arrangements were made for us to make the trip together. The day of our leaving, his wife was very tense about our going and stated that she was concerned that this many Black men could be together without something happening to the entire group. We decided to go anyway.

We had the very best accommodations. My brother James "Pap" Baker met us in Washington, D. C. James had flown in from Los Angeles and one of his ex-schoolmates had picked him up at the airport in D. C.

When we arrived at the hotel we made contact and James came to stay with us. We all arrived the day before the scheduled March because we had anticipated the capacity crowd and there were no hotel accommodations within 50 miles of Washington. Luckily we had made our reservation early and were within two blocks of the proposed meeting site.

The evening before the scheduled March, we were having dinner at the hotel and sitting next to us was a City Councilman from Detroit, Michigan. He stated that there would be 50 buses leaving Detroit at a given time in order to arrive in Washington in time because there were no hotel accommodations available for them. Also five planes would be leaving Los Angeles to arrive in time for the March.

By 10:00 a.m. the morning of the planned March we entered the grounds. Shortly after we were in place, it was announced that the Millionth person had entered and many more were still trying to get onto the grounds. These were the kindest most considerate people I ever met. We were standing and bumping shoulders with the people next to us and if one attempted to turn, others would have to also shift positions.

Those young people were so kind to my gray-haired brother and me. Several times they pushed themselves closer together to make room for me to kneel on the ground for a little rest then help me stand up when I needed to stand. They also fanned us with their hats to provide cool air.

I called home to Huntsville that afternoon and asked what had been said on CBS about the crowd. Back home the TV had reported there were about four hundred thousand men. It was announced shortly after 10:00 a.m. that the millionth person had entered the grounds.

It was an experience I will never forget for it was the friendliest most caring crown I had ever seen as well as being the largest number of assembled people. It was the GREATEST!

Wendell Baker and his brother, James Otis Baker, standing near Wendell's home next to "The End" sign on Baker Lane/Road. Photo courtesy of the Baker family.

Editors' Notes

1. Preface-- Mr. & Mrs. Scott Plummer (her given name not known) were friends and neighbors of Wendell Baker. They now live near Salt Lake City, Utah.
2. Pine Hill is east of Cotton Creek about two miles closer to the city of Huntsville.
3. Rev. A.C. Harris later served the Mt. Zion Baptist Church.
4. Iantha and Georgeanna Archie (Others' given names unknown).
5. Robert Nathaniel Dett, the first African American graduate of the Oberlin Conservatory of Music, was a renowned composer, director and educator in the early 20th century. He was at Samuel Huston College (now Huston-Tillotson University) 1933-1936.
6. The Reverend Maceo D. Pembroke later served the St. Mark Methodist Church (now United Methodist) in Chicago. A Northern Illinois Conference Ministerial training institute is named in his memory.
7. Wendell Baker was inducted into the U.S. Army March 12, 1944 and mustered out October 20, 1946.
8. Baker married Augusta Lee Jones of Victoria, Texas, in Neosho, Missouri, July 4, 1945.
9. Wendell Baker graduated from Texas State University for Negroes (now Texas Southern University) May 30, 1949.
10. Wendell Baker was an "on air" employee of KSAM from 1953-1961; for a short time he worked with then Sam Houston State College student, Dan Rather.
11. Jack Branch, Joe Teamer, and Paul Jones, calling their Trio the "Possum Walk Quartet" or "Baker Boys" sang at Wendell Baker's funeral service, November 19, 2013.
12. Baker began construction of his home on Montgomery Road in fall 1960 and moved in just after Christmas 1960.
13. Clyde Hall owned and operated the City Lumber Company in Huntsville in the 1950s and 1960s.
14. Percy Howard was the "new principal" of Samuel Walker Houston High School.
15. Baker's teaching contract with the Huntsville Schools was not renewed after the Spring Semester, 1961.
16. Wendell Baker began his employment with Goodyear Tire and Rubber Company in April, 1962.
17. Wendell Baker was hospitalized for four weeks in May, 1963. During his illness Baker committed himself to eliminating racist discrimination in Huntsville and the surrounding community.
18. The successful Walker County Voter's League was formed in December, 1962.
19. Huntsville schools began integration in the fall, 1965, eleven years after the 1954 Supreme Court decision, Brown vs. Board of Education of Topeka, eliminating school segregation. However, complete integration was slow; not until 1968 were the schools in Huntsville integrated. Pamela Baker, daughter of Wendell and Augusta Baker, was one of the first African American students in the previously all white high school; she also was the first African American student to graduate from Huntsville High..

20. Maxine Hayward, who had been refused admission earlier, was later admitted to Sam Houston State.
21. John Arthur Patrick enrolled in Sam Houston State in the fall, 1964.
22. Mance Parks succeeded Dr. Joseph Griggs as HISD Superintendent.
23. Huntsville Action for Youth (HA - You) affiliated with the Southern Christian Leadership Conference in 1965. James Bevel and Richard Boone were Field Organizers from the national SCLC office, and Booker Bonner an organizer from Austin. William B. Oliver was then Pastor of Plymouth Congregational United Church of Christ in Beaumont. Among the youthful civil rights activists were several graduate students in Theology from Southern Methodist University, including Milton S. Jordan, co-editor of this book,
24. Amos Gates was Walker County Judge from 1954-1976.
25. O.B. Ellis was Director of the prison system from 1947 until his death in 1961.
26. Brookshire Brothers, generally the African American community's choice for grocery shopping, was the store boycotted.
27. Mt Zion, in the Whittier Common School District, was several miles west of Huntsville.
28. Wendell Baker was elected to the Hospital District Board in 1979.
29. The Johnson/Goldwater election took place in November, 1964.
30. Father Al Johnson served St. Stephen's Episcopal Church in Huntsville.
31. The liquor election was held in 1971.
32. Jane Clements Monday was Mayor of Huntsville from 1989-1991.
33. Cecil Williams was elected in 1987.
34. Dr. Dorothy Huskey, a lifelong educator, taught and retired from Sam Houston State University. She died at the age of ninety one in 2009 at Knoxville, Tennessee.
35. On June 19, 1865, black slaves in Texas learned that they were free when the Emancipation Proclamation was read at Galveston. Since then it has been celebrated in Texas and elsewhere as a special holiday.
36. The "Party Machine" named William A. "Bill" Blakley in 1957 to replace Price Daniel and again in 1961 to replace Lyndon Johnson in the U. S. Senate.
37. Baker has conflated two separate U.S. Senate elections here. Senator Price Daniel was elected Governor in 1956. John Tower was elected to the Senate in 1961 after Vice President Lyndon Johnson resigned his seat. African American support was instrumental in Tower's victory over Blakley by less than 11,000 votes out of the 900,000 cast.
38. The Million Man March, October 16, 1995, was organized by the African American Leadership Summit, the Nation of Islam, and several other Civil Rights organizations. Estimates of the number of participants ranged from 400,000 to 900,000.

CIVIL RIGHTS ACTIVIST: WENDELL H. BAKER, SR.

Naomi W. Lede

By special permission the following has been taken from the book, *Samuel Walker Houston and his Contemporaries*, **written by Dr. Naomi W. Lede.[1] More importantly, I would suggest that you read Dr. Lede's book in its entirety to better appreciate our past history and where we are today.**

The process of school desegregation was set in motion when a newly-formed group, the Walker County Voters League, sent a letter to the Huntsville Board of Education. Recorded interviews with some of the community leaders provided insight into the mood of the period. One resident reported that "while the letter was being read to the Huntsville Board of Education, its members engaged in continuous conversations and paid little, if any, attention to its contents. When the presenter finished reading the letter, the Chairman of the Board stated that the Board would think about it." Following the incident, however, the Board of Education scheduled a meeting to be held at the office of the Huntsville Chamber of Commerce and invited K. H. Malone, Sr., from the Huntsville Negro Chamber of Commerce. Malone was asked to bring some other blacks with him.

It was reported that a plan was presented to the group for its approval. The plan "called for two or three black children to enter the first grade," according to several individuals. It was further revealed that the "enrollment requirements were stringent. Parents would have to first file a request with the black elementary school principal; if he approved, he would then forward his recommendation to the white principal. If the white principal approved, he would make recommendations to the Huntsville Board of Education. Following this procedure, the child would have to be tested, re-interviewed, and observed for personal appearance, and his or her ability to perform." It is not known how the "Special Committee" defined performance. Some viewed the plan as a deliberate act designed to restrict the number of children entering the previously all-white schools and to embarrass black children. One resident, now 75 years of age, stated that "obviously the plan was ill-conceived since most of educators find it difficult, if not impossible, to measure or predict intelligence, particularly when using the types of cursory measures recommended by the plan." Others felt that, at best, the plan underscored prevailing attitudes and stereotypical notions held by some local whites that black children were automatically inferior. White children were not asked to undergo similar types of processing and screening.

Despite the racial overtones apparently inherent in the plan, those who attended did not voice opposition to it. Instead, plans were made to hold a series of meetings with school personnel and community leaders.

First Meeting

Black citizens were notified of a meeting to be held at the Samuel W. Houston Elementary School for the purpose of "informing them of a plan that had been accepted by this Special Committee that had developed a desegregation plan." The meeting was convened by an elementary school principal. A huge crowd came out to hear about the future plans for desegregation in Huntsville. As the principal stood to address the overflowing crowd, a lone white man entered, took a seat, and began to make notations on a pad.

The principal stopped talking and took his seat. Individual citizens in the audience, observing this unusual action, looked back and began to ask, "who is this man?" This person came on the personal request of Wendell Baker who had taken this gentleman and told him how to enter and when to enter. Knowing the persona of this principal, it was expected that he would stop talking until this "strange white man" could be identified. The principal suggested that the person who invited him must introduce him. This man had been told to "just mumble some foreign" sounding name that could not be understood and that this principal would not ask him to repeat it. When asked to introduce himself, the white man stated his name and told the group that he had not been invited; that he had heard about the meeting and decided to come because he was curious to know, as a college professor, what blacks really thought about integration and opportunities for equal education in a community such as Huntsville. He further indicated that he "came down to observe and to make notes for his own good and for his classes." His name was not recorded because the audience did not understand what he said, and "was too embarrassed to ask him again." According to one community leader, the meeting was adjourned. The black principal stated, as he closed it, that another meeting would be called at a later date and that the Superintendent would be available to address the citizens.

Second Meeting

Several days later, it was announced a second meeting had been scheduled. Some concerned citizens contacted Wendell Baker, Sr., a graduate of the Sam Houston High School 1939, former teacher at SHHS, and a Chemical Engineer at Goodyear Tire and Rubber Company in Beaumont, Texas, and asked him if he would be kind enough to attend the meeting. Baker was one of the organizers of the Walker County Voters League, the organization that had sent a letter earlier to the Huntsville Board of Education.

The meeting was held at Samuel W. Houston Elementary School. One individual provided a vivid account of the incident. She recalled that "the Superintendent was supposed to present the outline of the plan for school desegregation." The number of persons attending was so large until there was standing room only in the auditorium. But, instead of discussing the desegregation plan, the Superintendent presented a demonstration on new equipment, and explained that it could be used by the District's black teachers. He praised the program at the black high school. The Superintendent gave a long discussion about the "fancy" equipment and, then, took his seat. Realizing that he had not solicited any input from the audience, he stood and asked, "Are there any questions about the integration program?"

One man attempted to ask questions about the so-called desegregation plan. Interrupting him, the Superintendent asked: "What do you want to know? What would you do over there (meaning, at the white school)? What do you want to go over to the white school for?" Without replying the man took his seat.

Following the first man's attempt to engage in dialogue about school desegregation, Wendell H. Baker, Sr. stood, was recognized, and proceeded to ask a series of questions. The dialogue went sort of like the following:

> **BAKER:** (Addressing the Superintendent) Could you tell me if the equipment you described is available to black teachers in the Huntsville Independent School District?
> **SUPERINTENDENT:** Yes.
> **BAKER:** Do teachers know about this?
> **SUPERINTENDENT:** Yes.
> **BAKER:** Has the equipment been used at the black schools?
> **SUPERINTENDENT:** I don't know.
> **BAKER:** Would you say that the equipment and other facilities at the black schools are equal to those at the white schools in the District?
> **SUPERINTENDENT:** They are the same.
> **BAKER:** What about equipment for foreign languages at the black school, would you say it was the same?
> **SUPERINTENDENT:** They have none.
> **BAKER:** What about equipment for foreign languages at the white schools?
> **SUPERINTENDENT:** They have the "very best."

BAKER: Are you telling these people here tonight that facilities are equal and that the equipment is the same?

Reportedly, the Superintendent went into a rage and told the audience that if "any agitator made the white people mad in Huntsville, they will have you all going to school under the tree." Observers stated that he further told the mostly black audience that "if any agitator in the community mess with me, I'll burn his toes off." Then, the Superintendent took his seat. The audience became enraged about what he said and the elderly citizens began to "mumble their disapproval." The Chairman of the meeting stood and asked if there were any other questions.

Baker interrupted and said, "Sir, I am not through. I still have the floor. I have not finished with my questions. The Chairman stated, "I am sorry, sir." Accepting this apology, Baker continued and stated:

> Seemingly, I don't have anyone to answer my questions, but I would like for this audience to know - the people who are sitting her tonight--that there is nothing at all to what you have been told tonight. We must think about the future education of our children; to train them so they can meet the demands of a society where the whole world is a community. These children will be required to function on a global scale. We can no longer live in just Huntsville alone. The world is growing; progress is taking place, and we must prepare our students for it. We, alone, must assume responsibility for our children's education.

Continuing, Wendell H. Baker, Sr. told the predominantly black community group that he was sorry that they came to hear "a program such as was presented here. The equipment is not available to black students or teachers." On this note, the meeting ended. Black community residents, walked one by one toward Baker to shake his hand and to thank him for having the courage to speak out about the future education of black children in Huntsville.

Despite the negative aspects of the community meetings, some black and white leaders worked together to create a climate for community acceptance of school desegregation. Although substantial progress was made in the development of plans to dismantle the dual systems of secondary and higher education, there remained considerable opposition to the general social climate in Huntsville and segregated conditions outside the school structure. A great deal of unrest manifested itself during the decade between 1950-1960. The Civil Rights Movement had its impact on Walker County.

Desegregation of Higher Education

In mid-1964 several black leaders became concerned about the slow pace of desegregation in Huntsville, particularly at Sam Houston State College (now Sam Houston State University). Two organizations—the Walker County Voters League and the National Association for the Advancement of Colored People—formed an alliance to deal with the issue of segregation in higher education in Huntsville.

Under the leadership of Willie Jerry Jones, Sr., and Wendell H. Baker, Sr., several attempts were made to desegregate Sam Houston State University. The first effort involved a female student. Once it was decided that the student would apply for admission, it was decided by the group that Baker would accompany Annie Lee Kizzee to the campus. They went to the Office of Admission and requested an application. Unlike other white students applying at the same time, the black student was referred to several people. After a number of telephone calls, she was finally advised to go to the Registrar's office. The registrar informed the student that Sam Houston State University "accepted white students only and, despite several suits in the State, SHSU has not changed its bylaws." On the following day, the Registrar followed up on his initial contact with the student by informing her that her scores on the Admission's examination were too low for her to be admitted to the institution.

In another attempt, a teacher at one of the schools in Willis, Texas applied for admission to SHSU as a transfer student In this case an entrance examination was not required. The Registrar sent her a letter "thanking (you) for your application" and stating that "we look forward to receiving (all required) materials." When the Registrar received Miss Maxine Haywood's transcript from one of the historically black colleges in Texas, he realized she was a black citizen. He immediately sent a letter to the prospective black student stating that "Huntsville was not integrated; that the community was not ready for integration" at the time. Based on these circumstances, Sam Houston State University would have to deny her "application for admission." Copies of the letter were sent to Wendell H. Baker, Sr., of the Walker County Voters League and Willie Jerry Jones of the National Association for the Advancement of Colored People (NAACP). They obtained legal counsel and a suit was filed in Federal Court against Sam Houston State University in 1964.

The Governor of Texas was out of the State at the time the suit was filed. When contacted by the news media and university officials, it is alleged that he instructed the Board of Regents of SHSU to desegregate its facilities. It is further alleged that administrators at Sam Houston State University took action immediately. The black principal at Sam Houston High School was contacted to enroll at Sam Houston State University. One observer reported that after several former students were contacted, a young man agreed to enroll. Arrangements were made to pay the student's expenses. On June 10, 1964, an article announcing the desegregation of Sam Houston State Teachers College (now Sam Houston State University) appeared in newspapers throughout the State and nation. The following account of the story appeared in the *Huntsville Item*:

> John Patrick, 18, 1964 valedictorian of Huntsville's Sam Houston High School is the first Negro to enroll at Sam Houston State Teachers College.
>
> The son of Mr. and Mrs. Curtis Patrick of Old Colony Road, Patrick is a chemistry major and will be studying mathematics and history this summer. Patrick's father is a long time employee of Boettcher Lumber Company.
>
> The Board of Regents of State Teachers Colleges announced a policy at a meeting in Austin last Friday morning that "a student is not going to be refused admission solely on the basis of race."
>
> Dr. Elliott Bowers, acting president of the College, at a press conference Tuesday afternoon, confirmed Patrick's enrollment and stated: "He (Patrick) is just another student and he will be treated like anyone else." Bowers went on to explain the Board of Regents' policy by saying: "We are now integrated." (*Huntsville Item*, June 10, 1964.)

Direct Action and Social Protest

The year of 1965 was a time when the drive for equal opportunity appeared to reach its peak:. There were massive demonstrations held throughout the South. Organized protests and boycotts were launched in hostile rebellion against racial bigotry and discrimination on city buses and in other forms of public accommodations. The Movement had projected the late Dr. Martin Luther King, Jr., into an unprecedented leadership role never before enjoyed by a black American; and had introduced strategies of nonviolent coercion never before employed on so large a scale in the Deep South.

The direct action movement aimed at changing the American social order had its impact on the Huntsville community. In March, 1965 a summer student project was developed, involving three hundred (300) students that were drawn from Texas' black, Mexican-American, and Anglo populations.

The project was designed to introduce students to techniques for political action and direct action (*The Texas Observer*, August 6, 1965). Following these efforts, the State AFL/CIO picked up the idea, reduced its scope, and arranged for a two-week conference for 75 students on the St. Edward's University campus in August in June, 1965. The Conference included, in addition to a number of labor speakers, both United State Senators from Texas and several civil rights people with experience in direct action. Among the latter group were the Reverend James Bevel of the Southern Christian Leadership Conference (SCLC), a key figure in the Birmingham movement and Booker T. Bonner who had precipitated the march on the Texas State Capital in 1963 with a 24-hour sit-in at then Governor John B. Connally's office. Several whites attended the meeting, including the Reverend William Oliver, a white pastor of a dominantly black church in Beaumont and two white students, Gilbert Campos, a University of Houston undergraduate, and Tom Lichten of Dallas, a Harvard University undergraduate. Four black high school students from Huntsville also attended the conference. They were: Andy Pope, Larry Jones, Karen Davison, and Gerald Davison, the latter two children's parents are: Mr. and Mrs. Kermit Davison of Huntsville. The elder Davison assisted at the conferences as a labor representative. Larry Jones is the son of NAACP leader, Willie Jerry Jones. The conference was moderated by Dr. William Cody Wilson, an associate professor at the University of Texas at Austin (*Texas Observer*, 1965).

In November 1965 Booker T. Bonner of Austin, Texas began organizing a civil rights protest group in Huntsville. A field representative for the Southern Christian Leadership Conference (SCLC), Bonner was leader of an organization called the Huntsville Action for Youth (HA-YOU). According to an article in the Houston Chronicle (November 14, 1965), the goals of HA-YOU were: (1) Complete social integration, (2) economics integration, and (3) to make blacks a part of the decision-making structure of the community. Bonner indicated that HA-YOU would work to get blacks hired in responsible jobs in utility companies, offices, and banks in Huntsville; that it would launch an all-out black voter registration drive. Assisting Bonner in his efforts was the Reverend Richard Boone, a veteran worker. Boone, like Bonner, was a field representative for the Southern Christian Leadership Conference; and both had participated in civil rights activities in Alabama with Dr. Martin Luther King, Jr.

The demonstrations at the Walker County courthouse, according to newspaper sources, prompted then County Judge Amos Gates to summon county road crews to demolish four brick patios on the courthouse square and remove public benches and chairs. Gates said he acted to "prevent trouble." He became one of HA-YOU's targets. Other targets of protest included the Life Theatre in downtown Huntsville and the Texan Cafe. Six young people--J.D. Gregory, Gerald Davison, Andy Polk, Charles Spears, Linda Johnson, and Willie Sowells--walked into the Texan Cafe and ordered, between them, two cups of coffee and one coke. After being served, the students decided not to pay the check and remained seated. They were joined by several white sympathizers, all natives of Huntsville.

They were Roland Eves, professor of Geography at Sam Houston State University; Sandy Richmond, wife of a sociology professor; Laurel Richmond and Ted Blanton, a student and president of the Young Democrats at Sam Houston State University. The two groups, each strangers to the other, sat quietly in the Texan Cafe. Eventually Kermit Davison, father of two of the demonstrators, went over to the cafe and paid the $1.28 check. (*The Texas Observer*, August 6, 1965).

After a series of demonstrations involving an estimated range of from 200 to 300 persons, including the one at the Raven Cafe, there was a series of arrests made. Twenty-six (26) white persons were taken to the Walker County jail, including Frank Pinkerton, professor of sociology at Southwest Texas State in San Marcos and Thomas Hipp and Wayne Oakes, students at Southwest Texas State; Hal Womack, a philosophy major at the University of Texas; Mark Klein, a student at Cornell University; Dick Viebig, a certified public accountant from Houston; Harry Schneider, a graduate student in political science at the University of Houston; Joe Hawthorne, a laboratory assistant at Shell Chemical Company of Houston; his wife, Mrs. Hawthorne; Rene Buller, a Beaumont student and son of a professor at Lamar Tech in Beaumont; Anthony Kneupper, a feed store manager from San Marcos; Margo Corley, an employee of the Texas State Institute of Child Psychology; Anne Keith Finleyson, a student at the University of Houston; Linda Shaffer, a University of Texas student; and Anya Allister of Berkeley, California. Also arrested were: Dr. Robert Stone, the Reverend Bill Oliver, Dr. William Cody Wilson, Tom Lichten, Larry Goodwyn, and a Mrs. Poteat. Elmo Willard, a black civil rights lawyer from Beaumont, was able to get donations of $5,600 to pay the cash bond to bailout the 26 whites at $200 each. The judge refused to accept the cash bond and required a property bond. Two Huntsville blacks, Mrs. Fannie Baker, mother of Wendell Baker, and A. L. Cox, put up a property bond in the amount of $5,600.

Nine (9) young blacks who participated in the HA-YOU demonstrations were committed to the Texas Youth Council and placed in the Gatesville School for Boys and the Crockett State School for Girls. These young people were among twenty-eight (28) expelled from Sam Houston High School and Scott E. Johnson Junior High School for wearing sweatshirts bearing HA-YOU emblems. School officials said wearing the sweatshirts violated a long standing school policy.

According to reports from school officials, the youngsters demonstrated inside the school. Louis Davis, the white principal at all-black Sam Houston High School, alleged that the demonstrations interrupted class-work and signed complaints against the students. Davis indicated that the youngsters were "disciplinary problems" before they joined the Huntsville Action for Youth. (HA-YOU) organization.

The demonstrations became intensified after the actions taken by Principal Louis Davis and then County Judge Amos Gates. Members of the HA-YOU organization walked daily picket lines around the Walker County courthouse protesting Gates' decision, racial segregation, and police brutality. According to Martin Dreyer of the *Texas Magazine* (January 30, 1966), the commitment of the nine juveniles to correctional schools for alleged civil rights offenses was thought to have set a precedent. County Judge Amos Gates, who judged them delinquents for "repeated unlawful assembly" sent six girls to the Crockett State School for Girls and three boys to the Gatesville School for Boys. Through the actions of an attorney, the juveniles were released a few weeks later on bond. Their cases went on appeal before the Court of Civil Appeals in Houston.

Huntsville was faced with a "dilemma of racial unrest." The dramatic and sometimes spasmodic actions had their impact on the climate of race relations. Marches on the courthouse, with college professors and ministers joining students; that cafe sit-ins, picketing, speeches and voices raised in freedom songs; the school demonstrations, expulsions from school, many arrests, jail sentences and fines; charges by the juveniles of police brutality and charges by a Huntsville photographer that he was slugged by a white man--were all part of organized methods to eliminate barriers to equal opportunity in social, economic, political, and educational institutions.

Bonner claimed harassment and brutality against him and HA-YOU members by the Huntsville police and the Walker County Sheriff's office. He wrote the late President Lyndon B. Johnson and charged that the Federal Bureau of Investigation (FBI), the U.S. Attorney's office and the Justice Department, and the U. S. Department of Health, Education, and Welfare had "refused to pay attention to the pattern of segregation in Huntsville."

Citizens of Huntsville, black and white, had mixed reactions to the conflict. Some whites held blacks responsible for Bonner's presence and activities. The black community was split in its attitude toward the demonstrations. For the most part, the differences in attitudes among blacks were related more to the methods employed than the problems and issues articulated. Some citizens questioned Bonner's tactics and his use of young people. Published reports indicate that Willie Jerry Jones, director of the

Walker County Chapter of the NAACP, disagreed with HA-YOU's tactics. He advocated a planned approach to change rather than symbolic and rhetorical gestures. Jones along with other leaders in the black community were extremely apprehensive about the students from Sam Houston High School who had been placed in state juvenile schools. Two other leaders, Scott E. Johnson, former principal of Sam Houston High School and Felder Jones, local businessman, became concerned for the students' welfare. According to reports contained in the *Texas Magazine* (January 30, 1966), several months after the campaign against "the Southern caste system" had begun, one of the girls, age 16, wrote her mother from reform school:

> Mother, I don't know what I have done to deserve this, but I thought I was doing what was right--and playing an important part in helping a lot of people. Can you tell me that I've done wrong? I keep asking God what I have done to deserve this.

As a former Principal of Sam Houston High School, having years of experience working with young people, Johnson's concern extended beyond the community to a concern for the lives of some of the students and their parents. He explained his feelings by noting that "it is a terrible thing he (meaning Bonner) has done catching the minds of those young people. The young students that were sent away, and others--I am afraid they will be warped because of it and it will handicap them all their lives." Continuing, Johnson asserted, "It is perfectly all right to picket, but what I object to is using children as fodder in front of this fight."

Willie Jerry Jones, businessman and graduate of Sam Houston High School, apparently summarized the feelings of those who opposed the strategies employed when he stated: "Demonstrate if it becomes necessary, but don't jump into the streets just for the exercise or without trying every method ... There are laws on the books now that years ago we never thought would be on the books at this time, and we should use them," evidently all blacks in Huntsville did not agree.

There were those who felt that Huntsville had moved too slow to integrate its schools and public facilities. More than ten years had passed, for instance, before the first black child was admitted to the first grade of a previously all-white school. Existing data indicate that by 1965 plans had been made to receive a few black students in the second, seventh, ninth, and twelfth grades (*Texas Observer*, August 6, 1965).

Some black citizens in Huntsville supported efforts to dismantle the dual system of education and public accommodations. Although judicially mandated by a series of civil rights decisions, Huntsville had not taken steps to provide equal opportunities for education and equal access to its public facilities prior to the demonstrations. There were blacks who bought food; furnished lodging, places for meetings; some provided automobiles for use by the demonstrators; others permitted their children to participate (even go to jail) in the interest of removing blockages to freedom. Local whites also supported the sit-ins and protests. It was reported that one white woman whose husband was a profound racist, called Wendell Baker of the protests and said she "couldn't let her husband know it but she will deposit in his mother's account in cash one half of all the bonds, which amounted to $5,600."

Against this background of protest, discontent, and exemplary black leadership, Mayor Raymond T. Wright of Huntsville who had been quoted in the *Houston Post* as saying "the less publicity given these things, the better," appointed a Biracial Committee. The Committee was similar in mood and composition to the one that had worked out Huntsville's original school integration plan. The purpose of the Committee was to negotiate to settle any differences that existed at the bargaining table rather in the streets. Through subsequent discussions and negotiations, some of the feeling of hostility sparked by the conflict and prevailing segregated conditions subsided.

Many who were living in Huntsville at the time of the HA-YOU demonstrations described the climate of the community as relatively calm when compared to "similar incidents that were occurring throughout Texas and the South at the time." Others were reminiscent of earlier efforts to plan for changes. Progress had been made relative to social conditions prior to 1964 when the National Association for the Advancement of Colored (NAACP) and the Walker County Voters League worked to alleviate segregated conditions, beginning in 1961 and extending through 1964. Under the leadership of Willie Jerry Jones, the local NAACP worked with some of the community's constituency to open doors of institutions that had been previously closed to Huntsville's black population. Following the HA-You demonstrations, the desegregation thrust continued and expanded to include Sam Houston State University. Among the participants in the negotiations for the admission of black students to SHSU were: Kermit Davison, Wendell Baker, Willie Jerry Jones, Mrs. Martha Walker Williams, and J. C. Phillips. Meetings were held at the home of Wendell Baker to discuss goals for the acceptable integration of all public facilities. As indicated earlier, the first black student, John Patrick of Huntsville, was admitted to Sam Houston State Teachers College in 1964. Facilities of public accommodations such as restrooms, eating establishments, motels and hotels, and public services were desegregated in the years that followed.

...

Wendell H. Baker, Sr. was a chemical engineer with the Goodyear Tire and Rubber Company in Beaumont, Texas. A former science teacher at Sam Houston High School, Baker is the eighth child of Jesse and Fannie Baker. His parents, Mr. And Mrs. Jesse Baker, owned and managed one of the largest farms in Walker County. Born November 13, 1922, Baker was one of ten (10) children in the family. Other family members include: Claude (now deceased), Alvin, Herbert, Frank, Jessie B., James, Nannie Lee, Wendell, Austin (Jeke), and Leola Baker. All of the children graduated from Sam Houston High School.

Baker's father was an outstanding civic leader in Huntsville during the 1930's and 1940's. Active in community affairs, Jesse Baker was a lifetime member of the Huntsville Negro Chambers of Commerce and served in numerous capacities until his death. An annual dinner - - The Jesse Baker Dinner - is held each year in honor of his contributions to the Chamber's development and to support activities of the organization. Wendell's mother, Mrs. Fannie Baker, was a housewife and strong supporter of school and community affairs. For her roles as mother, housewife, and community leader, Mrs. Baker was selected as one of the outstanding women in Texas in 1949.

Wendell H. Baker, Sr. started public school in the old Huntsville Colored School which was housed in the Old Andrew Female College building. The only high school at the time was the Sam Houston Industrial and Training School located in the Galilee Community. Children living in Huntsville had to transport to Galilee to attend high school. Baker's parents sent him to Galveston to attend school for two years. He was a pupil at the West District Elementary School from 1929-1931. Upon his return to Huntsville, he had to be advanced to the next grade, placing him in the same class with his sister, Nannie Lee Baker, because the books that were being used in the black schools in Huntsville in 1931-32 were outdated. He had used the books two years earlier He graduated from both elementary and high school with second highest honors.

An outstanding student in high school, Baker participated in the band and choral groups, including a quartet that won first place in State Competition. While in high school, he learned to play every instrument in the band. After his graduation from high school in 1939 he was unable to immediately enroll in college. So, at the request of Professor Samuel W. Houston, he taught music and served as interim director of the band until a teacher could be hired for this position at Sam Houston High School.

Later, Baker took a job at Belvin Hall at Sam Houston State Teachers College as a kitchen helper for twenty ($20) dollars per month. He worked seven days a week for five months, and saved forty ($40) dollars.

He received a tuition scholarship in the amount of $50 per year to attend Samuel Huston College (now Huston-Tillotson College) and became a member of that institution's dance band and choir. Baker also directed the Men's Glee Club. As a member of s sextet, he was part of a cadre of musical groups from Samuel Huston College that toured Southern California on a fund-raising trip for the private, church-supported institution. The groups also appeared at the Southern California Methodist Conference during 1940-41. These efforts were so successful until the school was able to pay its debts and to keep its doors open. The Samuel Huston Choir also toured major cities in Texas, giving recitals at churches and high schools as part of their recruitment efforts.

While pursuing his interest in music, he also demonstrated a keen interest in science, and was fortunate enough to study with the outstanding scientist at Samuel Huston College, the late Professor Frazier. During the years he spent in college prior to World War II, he divided his studies between vocal music and science.

He left college and returned home to assist in the management of the family farm during the 1941-42 academic year. Several of the older young men in the Baker family were preparing for a war that appeared to be inevitable. Changing world events had their impact in Texas as well as the rest of the nation.

By the time Wendell Baker graduated from high school, it was clear that the Second New Deal under President Franklin D. Roosevelt had failed in its effort to find compromises that would promote the interests of business, labor, and agriculture in common, and had become a farmer-labor government. It was clear, too, that the basis for World War II began as early as 1933 with the rise of two totalitarian ideologies-- communism and fascism, both of which were promising a higher standard of living and a renewal of prestige among nations. Both ideologists were direct opposites of what the democratic system promised to America and its allies. In 1939 when Baker graduated from high school, Britain and France had reluctantly declared war on Germany. By the summer of 1941 the United States was so deeply involved in the fortunes of Great Britain that a meeting between President Roosevelt and Prime Minister Winston Churchill was held to discuss pertinent world issues and to dramatize democratic objectives through the initiation of a so-called Atlantic Charter. Following this and other events, the Japanese attacked Pearl Harbor at 7:55 A.M. on Sunday, December 7, 1941. On Monday, December 8, 1941, President Roosevelt asked Congress to declare that "a state of war has existed."

Black citizens in Huntsville and other parts of Texas were affected by the events at the national level. Young men students at Sam Houston High School were required to register with local draft boards. Many volunteered to enlist in the various branches of the Armed Services. A substantial number of these young men had gained some experience through their participation in the various emergency relief programs that had been initiated by President Roosevelt during the New Deal era, particularly the Civilian Conservation Corps (CCC). Eager to serve their country, black young men at Sam Houston High School joined the Army, Navy, and other branches prior to and immediately after graduation. By necessity, some of the young men were needed at home to manage farms and families adversely affected by diminishing manpower and military separations, Baker, one of the younger ones in the Jesse Baker family, was among the three young men in Walker County to receive a farm deferment during World War II. He was deferred for two years.

In December, 1944 the Germans launched a counteroffensive in the West and broke through one of the weakest sectors in the Allied lines and plunged ahead along an eighty-mile front in the mountainous forested Adrennes region of Belgium and Luxembourg. The area, held by a thin line of solders, was under attack. Many Americans lives were lost in the Battle of the Bulge. The Adrennes offensive cost in Germans 120,000 casualties. Morris and Greenleaf (1969) listed Americans losses at 77,000 troops (8,000 killed, 48,000 wounded, and 21,000 captured or missing). The Battle of the Bulge was the gravest Allied military crisis of the war in the West. In response to this crisis, many deferments were rescinded. Wendell H. Baker, Sr. was inducted into the Armed Forces and trained for active duty in the Japanese invasion which began during the autumn of 1945. He was sent to Fort Sam Houston, Texas, Fort Lewis, Washington, Camp Crowder, Missouri; then back to Fort Sam Houston for technical training in the Medical Corps. Later, he was sent to Seattle, Washington and from there to Japan. Following the invasions, bombs were dropped on Hiroshima and Nagasaki and the Second World War ended.

When the war ended, Baker returned to Huntsville with the aspiration to become a medical doctor. While shopping in downtown Huntsville one day, he met and talked with Ottie E. Barrett whom he had known when he worked at Sam Houston State University in 1939. He told Barrett of his plans because he had demonstrated an interest in him. In 1939 when he quit his job to go to college, Barrett gave him $25 to help with his college expenses. As indicated earlier, he returned to Huntsville from service in the Armed Forces with a determination to complete his college degree and become a doctor. Barrett gave him good advice by suggesting that he finish his college degree, work for a while, and then consider medical school. Wendell Baker enrolled at Texas Southern University in Houston and pursued a degree in Chemistry. Two years later, he was the only graduate of the Chemistry Department the year he received his Bachelor of Science degree in Chemistry.

Meanwhile, Ottie E. Barrett continued to serve the Huntsville community after leaving Sam Houston State Teachers (now, Sam Houston State University). He was elected to the Huntsville Board of Education of the Huntsville Independent School District. Upon completing all requirements for the bachelor's degree, Baker visited Huntsville, and talked with Ottie E. Barrett. He told him that he was about to receive his degree and thanked him for his encouragement over the years. Barrett suggested that he apply to the Huntsville Independent School District. He did and was hired as a science teacher at Sam Houston High School for the fall of 1949. Baker taught all high school general science courses.

Teaching Experiences

As soon as he plunged into work as a teacher at Sam Houston High School, Wendell Baker had to face the bitter realism that the breezy promises of equality of opportunity for all were unfulfilled; that conditions had changed little in his hometown, particularly school policies and procedures that governed institutions for black children. School facilities were still separated and grossly unequal. A small elite group held the bulk of the power and decision-making positions. With this kind of consciousness, he began teaching with a tremendous enthusiasm and zeal. He taught general science courses to 9th grade students; biology to 10th graders; chemistry to 11th grade students; and physics to 12th grade girls only. When queried about this unusual arrangement, he explained that senior boys were required to be in Manual Arts (Shop) courses for two hours. They needed a class to fill the extra hour left for senior girls who were taking homemaking courses for one hour and needed an additional hour of course work. According to Baker, he had "an all-girls Physics course." They came to him for Physics and he carved a course out of his own experiences and educational training and creativity to meet their special needs.

Inadequate Facilities

With no facilities to teach general science, biology, chemistry, and physics--not even a blackboard, laboratory equipment such as microscopes and test tubes--Baker had to develop strategies for teaching that were inconsistent with the more orthodox methodologies. "There were no facilities at Sam Houston High School for teaching science courses--absolutely nothing in the laboratory," said Baker. Science classes were taught in the old Home

Economics cottage that had been constructed by "shop" classes consisting of students from Sam Houston High School. The building was so dilapidated that sewage would back up and manifest itself on the floor of the classroom.

Students in biology, chemistry, and other sciences had never seen a microscope before Wendell Baker began teaching them. During the period generally referred to as the "equalization movement" in school construction throughout the South, new black schools were built in an effort to remedy past inequities prior to the 1954 Supreme Court decision. The Huntsville Board of Education decided to demolish the original building which housed Sam Houston High School and construct a new one in another location on Highway 190 East. When the school was first opened, it did not contain adequate facilities for instruction in the sciences. "We moved into the new school," said Baker, and "for two years we did not have a blackboard and running water." Facilities were inadequate in the new school built after the 1954 Supreme Court decision, *Brown vs. Education*, outlawing "separate-but-equal" facilities in public education. Despite the apparent inadequacy of facilities for teaching science and other subjects, an illustrated report on the Huntsville Public School System (1954-55) contained objectives for the science program in Sam Houston High School that mandated modern facilities. The program's objectives included the following:

> The advancement of science related fields require that we equip our students with a knowledge and appreciation of science that will enable them to courageously face the problems of a changing world. We teach the students to appreciate the wonders of nature and life as well as develop skills in technical measurement computations, for these principles are necessary for a thorough understanding of mechanical and engineering skills.

It was unrealistic to believe that students in Sam Houston High School would be equipped to "courageously face the problems of a changing world" without the required equipment and facilities needed to understand the theoretical and applied principles of science. What was needed were facilities at least equal to those found at what was then all-white Huntsville High School. To meet changing requirements in science for secondary schools, a two-pronged attack was needed to bring the students to a level where they could understand and cope with changes in society.

The world had begun to change long before 1954. World War II led to a spurt in the use of rocket-powered missiles, which signaled the space age. As early as 1903 the Russian mathematician K. E. Ziolkovsky began publishing calculations which were the basis of scientific rocketry. He had proposed not only to launch earth satellites but to build space platforms as refueling bases for interplanetary travel. The V-2 missile had been developed by German experts during the World II, and Intermediate Range Ballistic Missiles (IRBM's) had already been produced. But, Sam Houston High School students lacked the necessary equipment and facilities for teaching general science courses.

Long past the dawn of the Space Age, Wendell H. Baker had to develop modified strategies for teaching science. The methodology to be employed had to be void of the laboratory equipment needed to apply the theoretical principles of science, chemistry, biology, and physics. When asked how he taught the courses; Baker noted: "It was difficult. We took the book, studied and analyzed the theories. We were thorough as we could be in theoretical rather than applied science. Students did a lot on their own. Parents were cooperative. The students bought their own materials. We made toothpaste, face creams, fingernail polish, hair creams, fingernail polish remover, tonics, hair growth oils, and similar compounds."

Parental Support

There was strong support by parents of students in science courses at Sam Houston High School. Children used their own funds to purchase what was needed to conduct experiments. "We concentrated heavily on the theoretical aspects of the sciences and this led to finishing the book before the year was over. Then we would just do projects, including baking cakes, biscuits, and other foods. I required the students to tell me the chemistry involved in each of the processes. We were not kitchen mechanics," stated Baker. The students had to read the theory, conduct the experiments, and tell me what every ingredient was there for, what it did for the biscuits, for example. This procedure was followed with all other projects. The students learned that way. Baker even experimented with some fermentation with ethyl alcohol because it was perceived to be a practical thing for students to know.

The students were highly motivated due to the innovative approaches used by Baker to provide instruction in the sciences. Baker became increasingly more concerned about the lack of applied science. While in search of a way to remedy the instructional disadvantages that were apparent, he took a trip to the all-white Huntsville High School where he borrowed a microscope from one of the science teachers there. According to Baker, he told the teacher, "Now, take this off the inventory because I am not going to ever bring it back. I am taking it to Sam Houston High School where we are going use it." Other equipment for the school was acquired through the efforts of Felder Jones, a strong supporter of the school's programs, longtime civic leader, and graduate of the Sam Houston High School class of 1932. Baker indicated that when he was in dire need of equipment he would talk to Felder Jones, Sr. about the things he needed and Jones would, in turn, mention it to the Superintendent. Through the efforts of Felder Jones, Baker was able to obtain some of the things he needed to provide adequate instruction in the sciences.

We found ample evidence of the effectiveness of his tutelage through students who chose science as a major in colleges and universities throughout the nation. Sam Houston High School produced more graduates in the pharmacy than any institution of comparable size in East Texas. Some of the students became science teachers; others became dentists and medical doctors. Prominent among those who entered the medical and dental professions were Dr. William E. Watkins, Jessie R. Wilson (Pharmacist), and Dr. Ulysses Watkins, Jr.

Crisis, Dismissal, and Recovery

Baker taught at Sam Houston High School from 1949-1960. During the latter year, he was faced with a crisis. He had to leave the Huntsville Independent School District shortly after he decided to build his present home. It was not a problem of economics; not a problem of choice; it was a situation where he was forced to make a critical decision. What happened to Wendell Baker, Sr. during 1960 was a clear indication of prevailing attitudes toward black professionals, the educational climate in Huntsville and community attitudes that influenced the behavior of its elected and appointed officials. The incident which marked the end of Baker's career as a teacher stemmed from his desire to improve living conditions for his family--nothing else. He decided to build a brick home on the property bequeathed to him by his late father, Jesse Baker. At the time, there were only one or two houses in Walker County that was owned by blacks that were constructed with brick or masonry. One was owned by Evan Shaw; the other by Dr. J. Arthur Johnson, a local dentist. Shortly after he began building his home, Baker was informed by the black Principal at Sam Houston High School that the Superintendent wanted to talk with him. Summoned to the office, Baker was told by the Superintendent: "Wendell, if you sell that house you built out there which is causing so much controversy among the white folks, we will give you a teaching contract for next year."

A native of Huntsville, the Superintendent, as it was told, succeeded Dr. Joseph Griggs. He apparently felt that black teachers should not improve their living status. Understandably, he was confronted with changes relative to school integration that were destined to occur; he was resistant to the ensuing social changes. Baker perceived his predecessor, Dr. Joseph Griggs, as a "man ahead of the prevailing attitudes of the community; a competent, good person." His successor, however, demonstrated attitudes that were symbolic of the segregated world of which he was a part. Supported by a power elite, his policies were apparently sanctioned by a school board consisting of members who had served on it for 28 years or more without serious political opposition. The general political climate in Huntsville was not conducive to drastic changes in the status quo.

The situation described by Baker bordered on "white surveillance." For example, during the time he was working on his home, five-to-six cars kept a vigil on his progress as he worked daily to complete it. He had time to reflect on the option that had been proposed to him by the Superintendent while he watched the cars, mostly occupied by whites, pass his house to get a glimpse of the project. Baker wasted no time giving his answer. His reaction to the proposal by the Superintendent was "I will not do that. I am building this home myself because I want my family to have a decent place to live and I will not consider selling this house." The Superintendent's reply was: "Well, we can't give you a contract--it's just that simple." Wendell H. Baker, Sr. was asked to leave the Superintendent's office and return to his classes at Sam Houston High School where he was teaching. He did not receive a teaching contract for the next year.

Unemployed and in need of work, Baker took positions with the New Waverly and Willis school districts as a substitute teacher until he was employed by the Goodyear Tire and Rubber Company in Beaumont, Texas.

His experiences prior to employment with Goodyear were interesting. According to his account, he took a friend to an employment agency to take a test and, rather than sit in the car while he completed it, he decided to go in the agency with him. The receptionist gave both men applications to complete. When they did, they were given a battery of aptitude, achievement, and personality tests. Baker scored very high on all tests, and was asked to wait and talk with a company representative. The company representative, impressed with his extremely high performance on the various tests, inquired as to whether Baker had attended an engineering school and the reply was "no." He then asked him where he learned so much about mechanics. Baker's reply was that he grew up on a farm, drove tractors; and did repairs on old tire tools and that sort of thing. Of even greater importance was the high score Baker made on the section dealing with knowledge on electricity. Confronted with his high performance on that section, Baker told the representative that he had been a science teacher and had taught some courses in electricity. The representative, obviously impressed by his knowledge in the field of science, told him that he made exceptionally high on all phases of tests. He was then offered a position at a very high salary; one that paid more in fringe benefits than he had made as a salaried teacher.

Following the interview he completed an application to Goodyear Tire and Rubber Company. Three days later, he was interviewed and hired to work at the plant located in the triangle area of Beaumont-Orange-Port Arthur in Texas. Upon acceptance of the position, he became the first black to work in a technical position with the Company. In April 1962, he was hired as an Analytical Chemist with Goodyear Tire and Rubber, and worked in that capacity for four years. Then, through a competitive testing program for engineers, he was promoted to Chemical Engineer because his scores were highest on the test. He held this position with the Company; and was a certified chemical engineer and a member of the American Institute of Chemical Engineers (AICH).

Community Affairs and Politics

The same courage which Baker exemplified in the field of education was transplanted to his role in community affairs and politics. Active in civic affairs in Huntsville and Walker County, Baker sought to explain the motivations behind his work in this regard. A series of developments spanning several decades impacted his life and motivated him to become active in his community. "I went to service," said Baker, "with no reservations about my country; with no doubt about the democracy of what I was a part. I saw young men who served just like me for a democracy that they had never really experienced. Yet, groups identified with the enemy like the Germans and Japanese were accorded full privileges in this country. They could eat in restaurants, sleep in motels and hotels, ride in the front of buses and trains; and use restrooms and other facilities. They could not even speak English, but could enjoy everything." This was really disturbing to me.

Continuing, Baker remembered that he returned to college at Texas Southern University when it was first established as "Houston College for Negroes." Later, the name was changed to Texas State University for Negroes. The institution had to use the facilities at Jack Yates High School in Houston to provide collegiate training for blacks. And, despite the filing of the *Sweatt vs. Painter* case, a legal challenge to segregation in higher education, blacks were not admitted to the all-white University of Texas at Austin. A separate and unequal university for blacks was established at Houston. "Those things touched me," Baker said.

There were also blockages, obstacles, and conflicts inherent in his teaching experiences that extended beyond the incident surround dismissal. "I came home and began teaching in a substandard building which had housed the Home Economics Department," revealed Baker. Faced with the task of educating black students in Huntsville, he was disturbed by an inability to get equipment to teach science courses; by the uncertainties surrounding buses when needed for field trips despite the fact that students paid their own money to participate. He knew that black students were being cheated under the segregated school system because he had been denied equal access to education. Reflecting on these experiences, Baker asserted that the could "never accept these things. I would take my students on field trips and I encouraged them, to be dignified. I helped them develop pride in themselves. I encouraged them to use regular restroom facilities not those labeled, "colored." Because of Baker's attitude in this regard, he was labeled a radical by some of the townspeople, but not by his students. He gained the respect of his students. Several, recalling those years, noted that "he voiced his dissatisfaction with the system and his students respected him for his intellectual ability, his concern, and his courage."

His challenge to the prevailing status quo was clearly evident in a situation which he faced involving a field trip to San Angelo. Baker wanted to take the students to see real mountains and to explain natural disasters associated with the environment to them on a first-hand basis. On the way back to Huntsville, the group stopped in Austin near the State Capitol to get gasoline and to use the restrooms and other facilities. There were three buses full of students. Having been briefed by their science instructor on a "code of conduct" to be observed, the students rushed into all restrooms while the buses were being filled with gasoline and checked for oil. One of the attendants at the gasoline stations stopped checking the oil, jumped down and went into the ladies' restroom and told the girls that they could not use it. Baker told the attendant that "if the girls could not use the restrooms, he could not use the station's gasoline." They drove the three buses across the street, used all facilities at that station, and bought gasoline.

These experiences and others had a profound effect on Wendell Baker. "Even when I was in the classroom, I was not an "Uncle Tom," Baker stated. He encouraged his students to get an education, and not accept a second class role at any price. As time passed, he became more determined to remedy the evils of segregation and Jim Crowism, and he chose his hometown as the territory where the struggle would begin.

In the community of his birth, he began a crusade to change it for the better. It was not a hasty decision. He had to think about what it would take to make conditions better for his people. He revealed that "it was clear that we would have to take the long way around. There was no short cut to it." The first step involved getting black people in Huntsville and Walker County involved the in political process. This required a massive voter registration effort so "our people could vote and determine who would be their leaders."

He relied heavily on the volunteer work of young people in the community, many of which had been his students. They were given bonus points each time they were able to register a certain number of people to vote.

Eventually a small group met with Baker and others to plan strategies for community organization. The plan involved pulling together existing organizations in the city and county. Though difficult at first, attention was directed toward elected or chosen leaders of groups such as choirs, usher boards, civic clubs, sororities and fraternities, the National Association for the Advancement of Colored People (NAACP) and others. The idea was not to supplant existing organizations or to co-opt their interests and objectives. Efforts were made to capitalize on existing leadership by pulling leaders of these groups together. No effort was made to change the interest and/or objectives of these groups. Instead, energies were directed toward common needs, common goals, and common concerns of the black citizenry of Huntsville and Walker County.

With a small group of representatives from the various organizations, the coalition began its planning. Others who were not in attendance during the initial organizational meeting were informed of decisions made there. Newsletters were mailed to more than thirty (30) leaders to keep them informed of the goals, purpose and objectives, and actions of the newly-formed group. These efforts resulted in the establishment of the Walker County Voters League in December, 1962. The group's primary concern was registering voters. At the time of its formation, a Poll Tax was one of the requirements for voting. Baker and his cohorts had to find ways to assist low income persons, particularly those on fixed incomes. A sustained voter education and voter registration drive was launched and it proved to be relatively successful.

The Walker County Voters League's work extended far beyond mere voter registration to engulf means by which the substance of power and control could be dissected. During the time when they were developing political strength, it was an established fact that Huntsville and Walker County had been controlled for a number of years by a small group of community influential, all of which were white. Historical data substantiate this contention. The sheriff, Floyd Farris, held office with little or no opposition for a period of 33 years. Former County Judge Amos Gates served his position for more than 20 years. Some of the members of the Huntsville Board of Education had a similar type of political longevity. An examination of the 1954-55 report submitted to the Huntsville Board of Education by then Superintendent Joseph R. Griggs, listed HISD's current and former board members. Board President Raymond Davis paid special tribute to nine members who had served the Huntsville Independent School

District "during the last ten years." Included were the following: H. R. Brentzel, Wince Smith, Roy M. Goolsby, C. Y. Townley, D. M. Phillips, Seth W. Dorrell, and Q. C. Robbins. The board members who were serving in 1954-55 included: Raymond Davis, James H. Anderson, Robert B. Smither, Ottie E. Barrett, Clyde E. Hall, Reed S. Lindsey, and Fred A. Bobbitt. Some observers in Huntsville stated that the school board elections as well as others were relatively routine for incumbents for several decades.

Beginning in 1962, the political climate in Walker County began to change. The Walker County Voters League targeted certain individuals for defeat. The County Sheriff was ousted from office. Observers noted that it was "time for a change because the Sheriff would not have been able to fit into the new era that had been ushered in during the 1960's; that his time had long passed into oblivion." Darrell White was elected to succeed Floyd Farris as the sheriff.

The Walker County Voters League continued its thrust for political recognition. In 1963 several individuals from the black community ran for political office. The black political candidates included the Reverend Iowa Jones who was a candidate for the Huntsville Board of Education; Willie Jerry Jones, Sr. and Wendell H. Baker, Sr., candidates for County Commissioners. Later, Wendell Baker ran for the County School Superintendent post; and Curtis Dickey ran for Constable. Scott E. Johnson and Walter Bibbs were candidates for City Council. All of the early candidates were defeated except Council Scott E. Johnson who served on the Huntsville City Council until his retirement in 1966. Curtis Dickey won an election later as Constable. Johnson was succeeded by Councilman Goree McGlothen, Sr.

In 1976 Anthony Branch, a graduate of Sam Houston High School, ran for the Huntsville Board of Education and was elected; then, reelected, and served several terms before his defeat in 1981. Another black candidate, however, was successful in the 1981 school board election. In an unprecedented move, Roxie Roy Douglas ran for the Huntsville Board of Education; was forced into a run-off election, and defeated her white opponent by a small margin. Her victory marked the first time a black woman in Walker County served on the school board. Mrs. Douglas, a former teacher at Sam Houston High School, became the second black to be elected to the school board. In each of these electoral campaigns, Wendell H. Baker Sr. played a key role registering voters, educating the electorate, and in providing guidance to the efforts of the political aspirants.

Between 1962 and 1981 another organization was formed to enhance the political activities of candidates who demonstrated a concern for the common good. The Walker County Council of Organizations was formed to support interracial political slates of candidates. It endorsed several white candidates for various offices along with black candidate, Richard K. Watkins, a graduate of Sam Houston High School, who ran for the office of County Commissioner and was defeated.

Wendell H. Baker, Sr. was serving his second term as a member of the Walker County Hospital District Board of Managers. It is an elective position that he had held since 1979. An outstanding graduate of Sam Houston High School, Baker married the former Augusta Lee Jones of Victoria, Texas in 1945. Mr. and Mrs. Wendell H. Baker, Sr. are the parents of five children, including Wendell, Jr., Pamela, Donald, Bruce, and Cima Baker. All attended Sam Houston High School. One child was born to Baker his first wife, Gwendola Crawford. His older daughter, Barbara Ann, is a teacher in the Houston Independent School District.

In the face of racism and economic, social and political adversity, Baker joined forces with other concerned leaders in Huntsville to improve conditions for citizens. The best summation of events that triggered the drive for civil rights came from Wendell H. Baker, Sr. as he reflected on the years he spent as a teacher. He taught twelve years at Sam Houston High School, beginning in 1949. In 1953, he was a Radio Announcer on KSAM and he held that post for eight years. In each of these positions he had experiences that impacted his outlook on life and general attitudes about social conditions.

As a teacher, he experienced blockages to his overall effectiveness by virtue of inadequate equipment in the classrooms. Black teachers were treated unequal in salary allocations and the amount of professional privileges allowed. They did not get sick pay. If they were absent from school, they would have to compensate the substitute teacher from their salaries. Black teachers could not drive school buses to make extra money. Yet, they received the minimum state salary. Baker recalled that his pay--after 12 years of teaching--was only $272 monthly. Funds paid by Sam Houston State University to the HISD for "practice teachers" were used for white teachers.

In the realm of community and civic affairs there were also inequities and general discrimination. Black policemen and sheriffs were assigned duties that involved blacks only. Other duties included transporting patients to mental hospitals. Chronically ill black patients had to use John Sealy Hospital in Galveston because of limited bed space for them in the Huntsville Memorial Hospital.

All facilities used by the public were segregated. When the new Sam Houston High School was built on Highway 190 East of Huntsville, the Principal was ordered to stop using Pritchett Field after it was learned that a football field would be constructed and located near the new site. When the Sam Houston High School Tigers opened the season the first year there were no bleachers for patrons to use; no press box from which to broadcast the games. Parents and students had to sit on cars around the sidelines.

Other concerns that prompted Baker to act included the lack of black employees at the Texas Department of Corrections (TDC) which is the largest employer in Huntsville. Steps were taken to integrate the employment force at TDC. Jobs were needed for the people. When actions were taken to negotiate the entry of blacks into the work force, the County Judge suggested that a plot was being made against TDC. Fearful of a concerted move to change the status quo, the County Judge got his maid's son to make application for a job with TDC, according to several sources. He did make application and was employed. In other actions, the Reverend Adair Holiday was appointed by the Governor of Texas to the Texas Board of Pardons and Paroles.

There were threats made against citizens and students who participated in voter registration. One student, James Earl Harrison, was fired by the Superintendent without prior notice when it was alleged that the young man had engaged in political activities. This action coupled with the aforementioned conditions served to induce Wendell H. Baker and others to take action. Typical of the prevailing mood of the time are the following words excerpted from a speech given when the civil rights protests gained momentum in Huntsville and Walker County:

> For generations now, we have been hunted down by whites and blacks alike and trampled into the red mud of despair. For what seemed to be unending years, we have tucked our tails and run like dogs from the heavy boot of evil produced by segregation. Our fathers and their fathers before them have suffered the indignation of having their manhood stripped from them before the very eyes of their wives and families.

The ideological position taken in the speech symbolizes the causes that impelled community leaders to take action. The essence of the causes is reflected this way:

> We have stood by meekly and let other men take from us the only thing that separates us from the animal, our dignity. We have rationalized that no manhood is better than death. Somehow, we have let ourselves grow to believe that living is the most important thing we can do. Well, I say it is not living but how we live that really counts. For generations, we seemed to be content with taking our problems to Jesus and telling

him that we are not getting a fair shake. For years, we have gone to the altars of the churches to find comfort, but I say here, that a man s soul cannot rest unless the body has a little rest also.

In an appeal to the grassroots level constituency in Walker County, the writer of the speech had this to say:

You see, a man is neither all spiritual nor all physical, but a combination of the two. And just as we struggle with the forces of evil to find rest for our souls, we must struggle with those outside evil forces to find the same type of rest for our bodies. And who among us will not agree on the fact that segregation is evil.

Acknowledging that "struggling was a tremendous job," black citizens and others in the area were challenged:

We must lift ourselves in every phase of life we possibly can. We must be strong economically, educationally, politically and mentally. . . . We must become somebody in the eyes of the only person who matters to us: OURSELVES.

We must develop political roots and become educationally strong. We cannot be educationally strong as long as we attend inferior schools manned, for the most part by teachers and administrators, themselves, products and victims of the same inferior system. And those who are worth their salt are teaching, not because they are dedicated, but because they are denied jobs in their fields in industry, management, and other areas.

We must openly refute those people who would scheme to keep us "in our places." And the best place to start is in our own community. There are those among us who will argue for "things as they are" and "not making Mister Charlie mad" because we have it pretty good. Well, these people are our worst enemies.

The speech ended with an appeal for assistance in a voter registration drive that was scheduled to take place throughout the State. The event marked the beginning of a concentrated drive to get black voters registered in Walker County.

A more in-depth account of Baker's role in the struggle for Civil Rights in Walker County has already been highlighted in the main text.[2] His values, anxieties, experiences, strengths, and future expectations are summed up in the following assertions:

> One's philosophy of life emerges from the sum total of his experiences. Each experience creates a crevice that determines one's desires, one's anxieties, impressions, disappointments, convictions; one's expectations, drives, dreams, and other contributing factors. The fight is constant. We have made a lot of progress, but the struggle is not fixed in time. Society continues to circumvent progress in human rights. We must stay politically involved; politically aware of the trends and changes in attitudes; we must learn the importance of working in coalitions; of working cooperatively with other groups. More importantly, blacks as well as other groups must learn the art of compromising: the art of negotiating the sharing of power. Information gathering and dissemination must guide our political behavior.
>
> Leaders must study the records of all candidates; hold the absolutely accountable for their actions; and circulate this information to those in need of it. The future role and participation of blacks in the political process, I believe, will comprise the essence of their survival and continued functioning in this society.

Editors Notes

1. Naomi W. Lede, *Samuel W. Houston and His Contemporaries* (Houston: Pha Green Printing, 1981), 176-186, 240-254.
2. Wendell Baker, *If Not Me Who? What One Man Accomplished in His Battle for Equality* (Huntsville, Tex.: privately printed, 2004).

DISCOVERING AN EXTENDED FAMILY

James A. Baker, III with Steve Fiffer

It rained on the cold November day in 2004 that I was supposed to give an outdoor speech in the Oakwood Cemetery in Huntsville, Texas.[1] That's where my great-grandfather, the first James Addison Baker, is buried, along with his friend Sam Houston, the general who won Texas independence, served as its first president, then—after annexation—as U.S. Senator and governor. The Texas Historical Commission had authorized a marker for my great-grandfather's grave, and I was invited to attend the ceremony to install the marker and say a few words.

Susan and I got out of our car and started walking to the cemetery under a dripping umbrella, when we were stopped by a very tall, attractive gentleman, who approached from the other direction. I had never seen him before.

"How do you do, sir? He said, extending his hand. "My name is James Baker."

"That's interesting," I said, playing along. "My name is James Baker, too."

"I know," he replied. "I have followed your career for a long time. I'm your cousin."

His name was James Otis Baker. Though born nearby, he had lived most of his life in Los Angeles. He quickly introduced me to his brother, Wendell Baker, who still lived in Huntsville.

I wasn't sure whether to take them seriously, but they seemed genuine in their assertion of kinship. In my remarks a few minutes later, I introduced my children and other relatives who were present at the event. Then, not knowing if I myself were serious, I introduced my "just-discovered cousins."

James Otis and Wendell Baker—handsome African American men—smiled as the crowd turned to identify them.

Afterward, a woman warned me to be careful. "That Wendell Baker is an agitator," she whispered."

"What are these called?"

It was Sunday, July 3, 2005, and I was driving through the woods just southwest of Huntsville with my newfound cousins, James Otis, eighty-six, and Wendell, eighty-two. Out the window I spotted a beautiful flower.

"They're called bluebells," Wendell said.

"May I pick one?"

"Pick as many as you want."

Jesse Baker was James's and Wendell's father, and their family still owned the sandy-soiled acreage and the old home place—off "Baker Road"—where Jesse and his wife, Fannie Willis, had farmed and reared their children. Jesse's father was Andy Baker, my grandfather's first cousin. Andy had had a relationship with an African American woman, named Emma Curtis, which made James and Wendell my third cousins.

They had told me about Andy and Jesse that rainy day the preceding November when I first met them, but they mistakenly thought "Andy" was a nickname for Robert Baker, a brother of my grandfather. They also invited me to attend the biennial reunion of Jesse Baker's descendants. I accepted, and that's how I came to be riding through the woods with them on a hot Sunday afternoon in July, eight months later.

Susan and I had arrived at Wendell's home about an hour earlier, along with two of our sons, John and Mike, and Mike's daughter Mary. (Some of my Houston Baker cousins showed up later.) It was a lovely brick residence on a large green lot shaded by towering pines. The living room walls were covered with scores of family pictures—formal portraits, wedding pictures, graduation shots—including one of a smiling Jesse Baker in a suit, tie, and hat. It was similar in style to the photographs of my grandfather when he was young.

I had had the family connection researched, and I explained what I had learned to James Otis and Wendell. "Your great-grandfather was Gabriel Baker," I told them. "Judge James Addison Baker and Gabriel were sons of Elijah Baker, whose grave I saw when I went to speak at a graduation ceremony at the University of North Alabama in 2002. My great-great grandfather Elijah, was also your great-great grandfather."

Gabriel had a son named Andy, I said. He was born in 1864, one year before the Civil War ended, and he would have been about twenty-three when Jesse was born in 1887. According to research done at San Houston State University, Andy acknowledged his son, wanted him to have the Baker name, and (by one account, which Wendell disputes) helped provide for Jesse until adulthood. (I have no way of knowing who is right about the question of support, but I hope Andy did that.)

When he grew up, Jesse farmed cotton and vegetables with mule-drawn plows, bought and sold land, and cut pulpwood and timber, James Otis and Wendell told me. "Everybody worked for my dad in the summer. He'd buy the land just to get the trees off it. And if he ran out of money, the bank wouldn't bounce his check."

Jesse had eleven sons and daughters, they told me. One was Herbert, who married a beautiful woman named Mackie. As a boy, I actually knew her. She worked for my grandfather, Captain Baker, and lived with her husband in Houston in a house behind the Captain's residence. The Houston Bakers "didn't know who she was," Wendell said. "We laughed about it."

My grandfather might well have known about Jesse because Andy is buried in the same cemetery plot with Captain Baker, who was his cousin. I don't know whether Mackie's employment was merely a coincidence or happened because she was married to a grandson of Andy Baker. One thing's for sure, however: no one ever told me or others of my generation of Houston cousins anything about this other branch of our family.

At the reunion, I couldn't help thinking about how much things had changed since my grandfather's day, and for the better. In the early 1890s, Captain Baker and other Houston leaders wrote a charter to establish what is now Rice University as a first-class institute for the "white inhabitants of Houston and Texas." That kind of overt discrimination seems foreign to us now, but it was standard back then and evidently what the founder, William Marsh Rice, dictated. University trustees went to court in 1963 and got the racial restrictions eliminated.

Wendell and Jesse told me with pride about their accomplished family and in-laws. Teacher. Lawyer. Judge. Social worker. Entrepreneur. Health inspector. First African American deputy sheriff in Harris County. Mathematician. Jazz prodigy. Network budget officer. Vice president at Disney—ABC Television Group. Marriage to a son of James Lawson, the intellectual architect of the nonviolent civil rights movement. (Lawson "is the guy who got Mandela out of prison and he is the one who taught Dr. King the power of nonviolence," Wendell said.)

As for Wendell's being an agitator—"and a troublemaker, too," he added cheerfully—that stemmed from civil rights work, including the registration of black voters throughout East Texas in the early 1960s and the peaceful integration of Sam Houston State University.

Wendell explained his motivation this way: "I said to myself, 'I have served in the army to defend America.' I said, 'We've been good citizens. We've been taxpayers. We're a productive family. Hell, I'm not going to take it."

One of his most fascinating stories was how he helped lead a movement in 1961 to throw African American support to Republican senatorial candidate John Tower. Conservative Anglo Democrats had locked African American and Mexican Americans out of the party, according to Wendell, and anointed a candidate he and other minority leaders regarded as a racist.

"Boy, we wiped 'em out. We put John Tower in there," he said. And afterward, "calling Tower was like calling my brother. He'd pick up the phone and say, 'What do you want?' We got blacks appointed to all sorts of offices."

I told Wendell and James Otis about having the support of several African

American leaders, including Barbara Jordan and Mickey Leland, when I ran for attorney general as a Republican against a conservative Democrat in 1978. "Barbara Jordan," Wendell said wistfully. "She understood."

Wendell then passed around a copy of his book, *If Not Me, Who? What One Man Accomplished in His Battle for Equality*. It's a fascinating read, including an appendix at the end filled with his aphorisms. "Make changes, but use the system to do it." "Compromise, but never when you get nothing." "Results count, excuses don't!"

In telling these political yarns, Wendell and I were not ignoring the likelihood that we had spent most of our political careers on different sides of many important issues. We were just doing what we should have done, which was to start our relationship on the basis of what we had in common, not what we might disagree about. At our ages, we'll probably never get around to the other stuff anyway, and it doesn't much matter whether we do. We did our part. The rest belongs to younger generations.

James Otis sat quietly while his younger brother told political stories, interjecting only once that I should have run for president. "I'll tell you, you did a good job," he said. "You know how to go and talk to people. You straightened out things."

On the way to the reunion, I had stopped by the family cemetery in Houston and copied the inscription off Andy Baker's gravestone. I now read it to his grandchildren. "They who knew him best will bless his name and keep his memory dear while life shall last." He never married, I told them. Jesse was his only child.

The reunion itself was wonderful. It was held a mile or so away at the home of one of Wendell's sons, Bruce, in and around a beautiful hardwood-shaded home down the hill from the main road. Out front, he displayed an old disk harrow, a symbol of his family's heritage.

When I arrived, barbeque was sizzling on big cookers, kids were running everywhere, and probably 150 relatives were swapping stories and studying a large board that displayed their family history. James Otis and Wendell introduced me to their sister, Leola. They were the last living children of Jesse Baker.

The day brought a swirl of emotions. A year ago, this branch of my family was unknown to me. Now Susan and I were being accepted with open arms and sweet spirits. I was profoundly moved by this experience and was pleased to have had the opportunity to learn about them and to reminisce with them about our mutual great-great-grandfather.

James Otis quietly shred memories of his beloved wife with Susan. Baker relatives came by, one by one, to shake hands, explain how they fit into our family, and welcome us. We posed for group photographs. Jokes were told. Children ran past, kicking up dust and wondering who these old people were. In these ways, two families acknowledged and embraced each other, becoming one family, quietly and happily.

Reverend Chris Bell, a great-grandchild of Jesse Baker, blessed the meal. "Holy Father," he said, "thank you for another opportunity for fun and fellowship, and for all those who have come such a long way . . . . Bless this food, Father God, that it would be nourishment to our bodies. In the name of Jesus, Amen."

Our hosts pushed us to the head of the line, and Susan and I stacked our plates with brisket, sausage, ribs, potato salad, beans, tomatoes, onions, and sliced bread. Then we went inside Bruce's home to enjoy our feast. In her lovely strawberry blond hair, Susan wore a single bluebell.

Editors' Notes

1. James A. Baker, III with Steve Fiffer, *"Work Hard, Study . . . and Keep Out of Politics!": Adventures and Lessons from an Unexpected Public Life* (New York: G. P. Putnam, 2006), 419-425. Former Secretary of State James A. Baker III included in his memoir this account and photographs of his first meeting with his African American cousins in Walker County and later joined them for a family reunion.

This photo, from July 2005, includes the four remaining cousins—Wendell Baker, Sr., James A. Baker, III, Leola Baker Adams, and James Otis Baker. Photo courtesy of the Baker family. The photo also was printed in James Baker's book.

APPENDIX

1
Points That Affect Me--My Goals and Resolutions

Make changes, but use the system to do it.
Compromise, but never when you get nothing.
Make the system work for you, don't be a victim by leaving it.
Results count; Excuses don't!
If your leadership is behind you, you're going the wrong direction.
A dead hero is no good. (To Anyone)
Results can always be measured.
When you relax and see nothing to do, your vision has a hole in it.
Seek advice only from those who have accomplished.
Change must have a reason--if not, create it.
Conflict begets attention: attention gets results.
The river is crooked in order to avoid opposition.
Life can't be straight if you avoid conflict.
Those who think there is nothing to be done are D.O.A. (Dead on Arrival) from their shoulders up.
Use obstacles as stepping-stones. They lift you up.
I believe I understand that the soul and spirit of man are immortal.
There should be a quality in one's life that arouses emotions called the Soul.
If the heart knew no weeping, it could not laugh. If the Soul felt no sorrow it would not grow.
What's more important? The life of your years or the years of your life?
Disposition of the mind is characterized by firmness and assertiveness is called Spirit.

2
Important Accomplishments

All through the involvement of Wendell Baker and the support of so many wonderful friends who have supported his adventures, the Huntsville community has changed a bit. A
few of the things that were accomplished because of him and others with him are listed as follows:
Abolishing of poll tax in Texas.
Lowering the voting age from 21 to 18 years of age.
Integration of Sam Houston State University (Annie Kizzee/John Patrick).
Integration of the Huntsville Independent School District.

Organization of the Ha-You Movement and chartering of it with SCLC.
Employment of the first Black by the prison system (Uriah Mayes).
Recovery of wages for cafeteria workers in the public school system.
Election of the first Black to the Walker County Hospital District.
Wendell Baker was the first Black to work in elections.
Established the Federal Housing Project on Martin Luther King.
Succeeded in having all streets in the city paved, including those in black neighborhoods.
Voted the city of Huntsville wet.
Voted in the Huntsville Hospital District.
Succeeded in have Avenue F renamed Martin Luther King Blvd.
Facilitated the hiring of a Black head of adult education program in Huntsville Independent School District (Cecil Williams).
Assisted in electing the first Black County Commissioner since the reconstruction era (Cecil Williams).
Assisted in getting the proper promotion for Huntsville's Black county agent (Mr. Epps).
Assisted in getting Huntsville's first Black principal in the public school after integration.
Assisted in electing Huntsville's first Black constable in Precinct @ (Curtis Dickey).
Started the City of Huntsville hiring only certified policemen.
Accomplished the integration of Huntsville Memorial Hospital.
Facilitated the rehiring of Black police woman Darsean Ford.
Accomplished the voting in of the Walker County Hospital District.
Accomplished the election of Huntsville's first Black city councilman since reconstruction (Scott Johnson).
Succeeded in electing Dr. Vickers to Huntsville City Council, who then introduced fluoride to city water thereby preventing tooth decay.
Succeeded in electing Blacks to county democratic committees.
Started Huntsville's prenatal clinic.
Integrated the Huntsville Public Swimming Pool.
Succeeded in establishing the 19th of June as a recognized holiday in Huntsville.
Elected and served for ten years on the Huntsville Memorial Hospital Board of Managers.
Served two years as Chairman of Walker County Family Violence Council.
Chair of the Texas State Teacher's Science Division. Local Chapter (Walker County) President of the Texas State Teacher's Science Division.

3
Certificates of Appreciation

Huntsville Greenway Project
Branding Iron Trail Riders Club Historical Project
Professor Carl Ross Historical Presentation Project
Kiwanis Club of Huntsville, Texas
Ella Smithers Geriatric Center
Walker County Hospital District
Sam Houston State University Alpha Phi Alpha Fraternity

4
State of Texas Certificates

Notary Public (Secretary of State)
Primary and Secondary Teacher (Texas Education Agency)
Public School Administration Principal/Superintendent (Texas Education Agency)
Surgical Technician (US Army Medical Corp.)
Medical Administrator (US Army Medical Corp.)
Chemist (Texas Southern University)
Chemical Engineer (American Institute of Chemistry-Engineering)

5
Texas National Resource Conservation Commission (TNRCC)

Soil Evaluation, Designing, Installing, Maintenance and Inspection of waste water systems by:
Texas A&M University Engineering Department
Leaching Chambers Systems of Texas
Hydro-Action Environmental System
Southern Aerobic Waste Water Systems
Cajun-Dir Waste Water Treatment Systems

6
Certificates of Training

Radio Technicians and Announcer
NAACP Leadership
NAACP Region VI Leadership (Little Rock)
NAACP Voter Empowerment (issue organizing - Alabama State University)

Voter Empowerment for African-American Farmers and Landowners (Tuskegee Univ.)
New Day Voter Empowerment (Alabama State University)

7
Certificates of Recognition

Distinguished Alumni, Samuel Houston High School.
Texas State NAACP Torch Bearer Award.
NAACP Million Dollar Club.
Walker County Council of Organizations.
United States Congress, April 16, 2001, Certificate of Special Recognition, Congressman Jim Turner.
Texas State House of Representative Resolution #499, March 19, 2001, Representative Dan Ellis.
Resolution from the Honorable Sheila Jackson Lee's U.S. Congress.
Resolution presented by the Honorable William Green, mayor of Huntsville, Texas.
Resolution presented by the Honorable Charles Wagammon, County Judge, Walker County.
Resolution from the NAACP presented by Gary Bledsoe, Texas State President.

SELECTED BIBLIOGRAPHY

Wendell Baker included most of these listings in the first printing of his memoir. The editors have added a few titles and some annotations to his listings.

Baker, James A. III, with Steve Fiffer, *Work Hard, Study . . . and Keep out of Politics*. New York: G. P. Putnam, 2006, 419-425.

Baker Family, Vertical Files, Thomasson Room, Newton Gresham Library, Sam Houston State University, Huntsville. Much of the information in this file relates to the first James Addison Baker and his family. He is the Great Uncle of Wendell Baker as well as Grandfather of James A. Baker III.

Baker, Wendell. *If Not Me, Who? What One Man Accomplished In His Battle For Equality*. Huntsville, Tex.: privately printed, 2004.

Baker, Wendell, "Working the Polls on Election Day." In Dan K. Utley and Milton S. Jordan, eds. *Just Between Us: Stories and Memories from the Texas Pines*. Nacogdoches: Stephen F. Austin State University Press, 2012. Pp. 123-125.

Baker, Wendell, et al. "About the Bakers." Prepared for the Baker Family Reunion, Escondido, California, July 3, 4, 1999. In possession of the Baker family, Huntsville.

Baker, Wendell. Interview by Bernadette Pruitt, February 1, 2003. Tape recording in Possession of the Baker family, Huntsville.

Bryant, Ira B. *Texas Southern University: Its Antecedents, Political Origins and Future*, Houston: Self Published, 1975.

Buckley, Gail, *American Patriots: The Story of Blacks in the Military from the Revolution to Desert Storm*, New York: Random House, 2001.

Dalfume, Richard M. "Forgotten Years of the Negro Revolution," *Journal of American History*, 55 (June 1968), 90-106.

Dwyer, Charles L., and Gerald L. Holder. "Huntsville, Texas," *The New Handbook of Texas*, Vol. 3, Austin: Texas State Historical Association, 1996

Freeman, J. H. "James Addison Baker" *The New Handbook of Texas*, 1, Austin: Texas State Historical Association, 1996.

_____. "Baker and Botts," *The New Handbook of Texas*, Vol 1, Austin: Texas State Historical Association, 1996.

Glasrud, Bruce A., and Archie P. McDonald, eds. *Blacks in East Texas History*. College Station: Texas A & M University Press, 2008. Many of the essays in this volume cover directly or indirectly, the issues Baker confronted in his Civil Rights struggle.

Glasrud, Bruce A., and James M. Smallwood, eds. *The African American Experience in Texas*. Lubbock: Texas Tech University Press, 2007.

Goodwyn, Larry. "Hey-You in Huntsville," *The Texas Observer* (August 6, 1965), 1-9. Goodwyn subtitled this report "Novel Tactics in the Campaign Against the Southern Caste System--A Participant's Report on Militant Negroes Winning Integration and Whites Going to Jail in Support of Them."

Baker, who was actively involved in the campaign, is mentioned in the first sentence and often in Goodwyn's report. Other issues of the *Observer* at this time have further accounts of similar events in Walker County and throughout the state.

Goodwyn, Lawrence C. "Populist Dreams and Negro Rights: East Texas as a Case Study," *The American Historical Review* 76.5 (Dec. 1971) 1435-1456. By 1971 Goodwyn had left the Observer and was Assistant Professor of History at Duke University. Although this essay does not deal with Wendell Baker or events in Walker County, Goodwyn makes a strong case for the importance of hearing minority voices, such as Baker's, rather than relying solely on the voices of the established community in writing the history of Civil Rights struggles.

Halberstam, David. *The Children*. New York: Fawcett, 1999. Thus book depicts the efforts of Rev. Dr. James Lawson with the Nashville sit-in movement.

Hine, Darlene Clark, *Black Victory: The Rise and Fall of the White Primary in Texas*. Milwood, NY: Kraus Thompson, 1974. Reprinted in 2006 by University of Missouri Press. Efforts to deny African Americans a voice in the political process continued in Texas well past the days of the White Primary. Securing the vote for African Americans was a primary focus of much of Baker's activity.

_____. *African American Odyssey*. 2nd edition. Upper Saddle River, NJ: Prentice Hall, 2003. Baker included this study by Hine in his bibliography, though not the study of the white primary above.

Horace, Lillian Jones. *Five Generations Hence, in Recovering Five Generations Hence: The Life and Writings of Lillian Jones Horace*. Edited by Karen Kossie-Chernyshev. College Station: Texas A&M University Press, 2013. Pp. 11-102.

John, Cheval. "Wendell Baker: The Martin Luther King of Huntsville" (http://vallanomedia.com/2011/02/01/wendell-baker).

Lede, Naomi W. *Samuel Walker Houston and His Contemporaries: A Comprehensive History of the Origin, Growth and Development of the Black Education Movement in Huntsville and Walker County*, Houston: Pha Green Printing, 1981. Baker was a student at Samuel Walker Houston's school and later a teacher in the segregated high school in Huntsville that bore Houston's name. Dr. Lede included a lengthy account of Baker's activities in her study. With permission he included a portion that is also included here.

Leffler, John, "Walker County" *The New Handbook of Texas*, Vol. 6, Austin: Texas State Historical Association, 1996.

Littlejohn, Jeff. "Democracy and Diversity in Walker County, Texas" (http://www.studythepast.com/democracy/personnel.htm).

Lucko, Paul M. "Samuel W. Houston," *The New Handbook of Texas*, Vol 3, Austin: Texas State Historical Association, 1996.

May, James, "Texas Legislature," *The New Handbook of Texas*, Vol 6, Austin: Texas State Historical Association, 1996.

Prather, Patricia S. and Jane C. Monday, *From Slave to Statesman: The Legacy of Joshua Houston, Servant of Sam Houston*, Denton: University of North Texas

Press, 1993. Joshua Houston was a leader of the African American Community in Huntsville and Walker County during Reconstruction and the father of Samuel Walker Houston.

Pratt, Joseph and Kenneth Lipartito. *Baker and Botts and the Development of Modern Houston*. Austin: University of Texas Press, 1991. The Baker and Botts law firm was founded by the first James Addison Baker who was the Grandfather of James A. Baker III and Great Uncle of Wendell Baker. It was at an Historical Marker dedication for the elder J. A. Baker that Wendell Baker and his brother, James, first met James A. Baker III.

Pruitt, Bernadette, "For the Advancement of the Race: African American Migration and Community Building in Houston, 1914-1945," PhD dissertation, University of Houston, 2001. A revised version of this dissertation, *The Other Great Migration: The Movement of Rural African Americans to Houston, 1900-1941*, was published by Texas A and M University Press in 2013. Dr. Pruitt, now Associate Professor of History at Sam Houston State University, Huntsville, worked closely with Wendell Baker to inform her students and many others of the Civil Rights struggles in the region in the mid-20th century.

_____. "Wendell Baker and the Civil Rights Movement in Huntsville, Texas" (http://studythe past.com/democracy/Wendell_ Baker_home.htm).

Pruitt, Bernadette. and Naomi W. Lede. "Wendell H. Baker, Sr." I*n Pathfinders: A History of the Pioneering Efforts of African Americans, Huntsville, Walker County, Texas*. Edited by Naomi W. Lede. Virginia Beech, Vir.: Donning Company Publishers, 2004. Pp. 155-157.

Sosebee, Scott. "Wendell Baker: Fighting for Rights for Sixty Years." *The Daily Sentinel* (Nacogdoches). November 24, 2013.

Walker County Historical Commission, *Walker County: A History*, Huntsville: The Walker County Historical Commission for the Walker County Genealogical Society, 1986. Most of the entries in this history, focused primarily on the majority community, are written by family members or close friends.

Williams, David. "A Brief History of St. James Methodist Church," in possession of the Baker family, Huntsville. Joshua Houston, father of Samuel Walker Houston, was a founding member and Trustee of St. James.

Zellar, Gary. "The Integration of Huntsville Independent School District, 1954-1965," Masters Thesis , Sam Houston State University, 1994. Pamela Baker, daughter of Wendell and Augusta Baker, was one of the first African American students to enroll in the previously all white Huntsville High School.

INDEX

Wendell Baker included this index to his memoir in the first printing. The editors have made the changes necessary for this new edition

Adams, Leola Baker	62
Adams, Jesse (Sonny)	62
AFL-CIO	77
Archie Sisters, Iantha, Georgiana	28
Archie, Toy	48
Atlanta, Georgia	35, 65
Austin	36
B.F. Goodrich	40
Baines, William	36
Baker, Augusta Lee Jones	32, 68
Baker Boys	25
Baker, Cima	65
Baker, Claude	38
Baker, Herbert	32, 38
Baker, James (PAP)	32, 79
Baker, Jesse	24, 26, 41
Baker, Nannie Lee	29
Baker, Pamela Joyce	65
Baker, Wendell Sr.	24, 50
Baker, Wendell Jr.	79
Barrett, Ottie	34
Beaumont, Texas	31, 40, 42, 46, 49
Belvin Hall	29, 30
Beseda, Buster	42
Bevel, Rev. James	47
Black Legislative Caucus	76
Black Republicans	58
Blasik, Frank	65
Boone, Rev. Richard	47
Bonner, Booker T.	47
Branch, Anthony (Jack)	36
Bronze Variety Hour	35
Brown vs Board of Education	35, 45, 46
Bush, Ebenezer	32-33
Camp Crowder, MO	32
Campos, Gilbert	47

Carver, Dr. George Washington	33
C.B.S.	35, 79
Chrietien, Florence Glen	29
Cliborne, Robert M.	40
Crooks, Sonny	48
Crosby, Bing	31
Daniel, Senator Price	77
Dett, R. Nathaniel	30
Dickie, Curtis (Jab)	71
Dupont	40
Ellis, O.B.	47
East Texas Citizens League	77
Epps, Hugh	60
Felder Dry Goods	42
Felder, Jack	42
Ferguson Sisters	28
Firestone Rubber Co.	40
Ford, Dineen	67
Fort Lewis, Washington	32
Fort Sam Houston	32-33
Franklin, Jimmie	35
Frazier, Mason Steele	29, 30
Future Farmers of America	35
Gates, Amos (County Judge)	47
Glaze, John Henry	36
Goldwater, Barry	50
Goodyear Tire & Rubber Co,	40, 43
Greater Zion Baptist Church	36
Gregory, J.D.	47
Griggs, Dr. Joseph	45
Grover, Brother and Sister	28
Grover, Ernest	61
Gulf Oil	40
Hall, Clyde	38
Harris, A,C.	26
Harris County Council pf Organizations	77
Harrison, James Earl	36
Harvard University	47
Ha-You (Huntsville Action for Youth)	47
Hayward, Maxine	44
Helms Bakery	31

Hightower, Lou (Tip)	40
Hope, Bob	31
Hospital District Board of Managers	50
Houston, Samuel Walker	28-29
Houston, University of	47
Howard University	47
Huffer, Dr. Earl	45
Huntsville/Walker County Chamber of Commerce	45-46
Huntsville City Council	53
Huntsville Independent School District	59, 42, 49
Huntsville Independent School District Black Cafeteria Workers	53
Huntsville Independent School District Challenge Program	63
Huntsville Memorial Hospital	68-69
Huskey Dr. Dorothy	69
Japan	32
Johnson, Father Al	50
Johnson, Lyndon B. (U.S. President)	50
Johnson, Scott E.	70
Jones, Billy Ray	36
Jones, Lynn	36
Jones, Paul	36
Jones, Willie Jerry	68
King, Dr. Martin Luther Jr.	47, 56
Kizzie, Annie Lee	44
KSAM	65
Lamar University	47
Lichtin, Thomas	47
Mayes, Uriah	47
Maxey, Waydell	36
Merchant, Bobby	36
McGowan, George	36
Million Man March	79
Mobil Oil	40
Monday, Jane (Mayor)	56
Moore, Bill (Senator)	45, 76
Moore, Bradley	29
Mr. V.C.	38
Mosley, Ruthie Lee	48
Murray, Earl	35-36

NAACP	56
National Science Foundation	35
New Farmers of America (N.F.A.)	35, 38
Oliver, William B. (Rev.)	47
Owens, Edward	53
Owens, Hattie	53
Park, Mance	42
Patrick, John A.	44-45
Pearl Harbor	35
Pembroke, Maceo	31
Perry, George	56
Phillips, J.C.	53
Plummer, Scott	23
Prairie View A&M University	29, 32, 58
Pure Oil	40
Rather, Dan	35
Republicans of Walker County	58
Robinson, Jackie	31, 40
Robinson, Wilburn	68
Rogers, Howard M.	36
Rolling, Moultie	53
Roosevelt, Franklin D. (U.S. President)	32
Ross, Floyd	53
Sam Houston High School	29-30, 34
Sam Houston State Teacher's College	29, 34
Sam Houston State University	35, 44
Samuel Huston College	29-30
Samuel Walker Houston High School	28, 34, 47
San Jacinto Battleground	37
S.C.L.C. (Southern Christian Leadership Conference)	47
Smith, Calvin	35
Smith, Sammie	36
Southern California Methodist Conference	31
Sweat, Heman	34
Teamer, Joe	36
Texas Black Republicans	77
Texas Council of Voters	77
Texas Democratic Machine	77
Texas State University for Negroes	34
Texas Southern University	34
Thiegpen, Lee A. (Rev.)	42

Tolliver, T.L.	36
Tower John (Senator)	77-78
Tuskegee University	33
United Negro College Fund	31
University of Texas	31, 34
University of Texas Medical Branch	50
U.S. Department of Education	42, 45
U.S. Department of Labor	48
Veterans Administration	37
Vickers, Dr. Frank	72
Walker County Clerk's Office	41, 42
Walker County Democratic Chair	51-52
Walker County School Superintendent	48
Walker County School Trustees	48
Walker County Voters League	42, 47-48, 53, 56, 69
Watkins, Richard K.	56
West District School	28
White, Darrell (Sheriff)	62
Williams, Cecil	56, 58
Williams, Hattie	28
Williams, John	36
Williams, Lester	58
Williams, Maggie	58
Willis, Fannie	23
Willis, Frank	26
Willis, Lucy Mason	53
Wilson, Woodrow	38
Woodall, Ross	52
Young, Tommy	36

www.ingramcontent.com/pod-product-compliance
Lightning Source LLC
Chambersburg PA
CBHW061233070526
44584CB00030B/4098